An Exploration into the Destiny of the

of the

Waldorf School Movement

An Exploration into the Destiny of the Waldorf School Movement

by

Frans Lutters

Translated by
Philip Mees

Waldorf PUBLICATIONS

RESEARCH INSTITUTE FOR *Waldorf* EDUCATION

Printed with support from the Waldorf Curriculum Fund

Published by:
Waldorf Publications at the
Research Institute for Waldorf Education
38 Main Street
Chatham, NY 12037

Title: *An Exploration into the Destiny of the Waldorf School Movement*
Author: Frans Lutters
Translator (from Dutch): Philip Mees
Editor: David Mitchell
Copy Editor and Proofreader: Ann Erwin
Cover: David Mitchell
© 2011 by AWSNA
Reprinted 2015 by Waldorf Publications
ISBN # 978-1-936367-19-1

TABLE OF CONTENTS

PREFACE

*T*his book is the result of research I have done over the past several decades into the destiny of the Waldorf school movement. It collects the articles I have published on the subject in *Letters to Teachers* for the Waldorf teachers in Holland and in the periodical *Vrije Opvoedkunst (The Art of Free Education)*. Again and again I have been asked to collect these letters into a book, but this was not possible until the project had come to a certain conclusion. This has now happened, and I am happy that this collection could become part of the spiritual life of the Waldorf school movement in The Netherlands during the Michaelmas Conference for Waldorf schools 2004, and now more worldwide in this English publication.

In this preface I want to thank those who have made this book possible. Rob Tuk did a lot of work for it and dedicated himself to it with never flagging enthusiasm. Many thanks to him. I also want to thank Roelof Jan Veltkamp and the editors of *Letters to Teachers* for their repeated processing and publication in the course of the past twelve years of the articles collected here. Finally, I want to thank Philip Mees for his translation and the work he did for making this study available for a broader readership.

I hope this book may help create a greater awareness of the historical source of Waldorf school pedagogy, and that it may also be a source of inspiration for the work in these schools. Its purpose is not so much to communicate information, but more to present content for inner deepening.

Because every chapter was originally published as a separate article, there is some repetition of certain themes. However, when this occurs the context is always different, so that the theme is presented from a different point of view.

– Frans Lutters
Michaelmas 2011

INTRODUCTION

THE WALDORF SCHOOL MOVEMENT IN THE LIGHT OF THE NINTH CENTURY

*I*n 1974 one of the founders of the first Waldorf school in The Netherlands, Daniel van Bemmelen, gave a lecture at the Free Pedagogical Academy (the Dutch Waldorf teachers training college) in which he called attention to the connection of the pedagogical impulse living in Waldorf schools with developments in Carolingian times. "The karma of the Dutch Waldorf school is part of the world karma that underlies the first Waldorf school founded in Stuttgart [Germany in 1919]. If we want to find the origin of this karma we have to go back to the 8th and 9th centuries, the time of Charlemagne who lived from 742–814."

He discusses how Charlemagne received the impulse to found schools in his realm from his mother, Berta, also called Bertrada. This woman is 'Goosefoot Berta' (*Berta aus grans pieds*) who lives on in Middle-European spiritual life in the fairy tales she was the first to tell: the fairy tales of Mother Goose.

In order to realize this pedagogical impulse, which is expressed in the founding of public schools and universities, Charlemagne brought together scientists, priests and artists from all over Europe. In these schools the students were taught not only in Latin, but also in the local vernacular. Side by side with the arts of writing and arithmetic, Charlemagne put great importance on the practice of music, especially singing. This impulse toward founding schools must therefore be viewed as the origin of the world karma that underlies the Waldorf school movement. Although it was for Charlemagne a straightforward, unified impulse, in the scholars, priests and artists he collected around himself two different streams could be distinguished.[1]

We owe it to the trailblazing work of Walter Johannes Stein that we are able to get a clearer view of these two streams around Charlemagne. In his book *The Ninth Century* they become visible. One is more Roman-Christian oriented, the other more Irish-Christian. In the 8th century Irish Christianity still had a cosmic orientation and experienced the Christ impulse out of a certain clairvoyant perception. By contrast, Roman Christianity considered every clairvoyant perception as a threat for the development of the emerging intellect. We see that Charlemagne stood in the midst of the growing tension between these two streams, and that in the course of time the Roman stream would drive out the Irish one.

But let us return to Charlemagne. In his time it was a most unusual pioneering deed for a king (for he was then not yet emperor) to become the founder of public schools open to ordinary people. We find this same characteristic in the founding of the first Waldorf school in Stuttgart, Germany, by Emil Molt in 1919. Just as it was unusual in Carolingian times for a king to found public schools, it was just as unusual early in the

Emil Molt

20th century for a factory owner/manager to found a school for the education of children of workers together with children from higher social classes.

Charlemagne at 26 years

Charlemagne received the impulse from his mother Berta. Her father, and therefore Charlemagne's grandfather on his mother's side, was Charibert de Laon. This personality hides an important Christian initiate. In the German saga of Flor and Blanchefleur, he is identified as Flor, about whom Steiner once said in all openness: "The same soul that lived in Flor appeared again in the 13th and 14th centuries to found a new mystery school that would protect the Christ secret in a way that was appropriate for the New Era. He became the founder of Rosicrucianism."[2] This founder is known under the name of Christian Rosenkreutz.

Berta, daughter of Charibert de Laon, carried this deep Christian impulse which she received from her father. Out of this impulse she urged her son to found schools for the common people. Just as in the 8th century Christian Rosenkreutz stood at the cradle of the schools founded by Charlemagne, in the same way Steiner stood at the cradle of the first Waldorf school founded by Emil Molt. In the spiritual world Rudolf Steiner and Christian Rosenkreutz work very closely together. The Waldorf school movement can make itself conscious of the connection it has with both these great Christian initiates.

In his autobiography Emil Molt relates how, in the years when the Waldorf-Astoria factory grew into a large enterprise, he and his wife Berta met Steiner, and how they both knew during a lecture on the Gospel of St. John that for the rest of their lives they could have complete confidence in what this human being told them. The collaboration between Emil Molt and Rudolf Steiner became especially intensive during World War I when Molt attempted to make genuine spiritual-scientific insights in the causes of the war known in military circles. In 1917 Steiner wrote for the first time about the threefold constitution of the human being, and at about the same time the movement promoting the threefold social order arose, something with which Emil Molt was deeply involved.

This is only a summary review to show how in this incarnation Emil Molt carried the destiny of Europe in his heart. The foundation of the Waldorf school movement was the crown on these intentions. Old karma became new karma in the founding of the first Waldorf school.

Charlemagne

2

THE QUESTION OF THE KARMA OF THE WALDORF SCHOOL MOVEMENT

$\mathcal{T}$ he picture of the threefold human being forms the source of inspiration for our pedagogic activity in Waldorf schools. In the lectures Rudolf Steiner gave to the first Waldorf teachers, he again and again emphasized the threefoldness of the human being as a central theme.[3] This threefoldness can be directly experienced in our thinking, feeling and will. In addition we have a threefoldness in our physicality, namely our head, chest and limbs. And in the overarching threefoldness of body, soul and spirit we find a true image of the human being. The differentiation of the human being as to body, soul and spirit disappeared from European culture in the 9th century.

At the Council of Constantinople in 869 AD the distinction between soul and spirit was abolished. From that moment the authority of the Church acknowledged only that the soul had certain spiritual characteristics. This resulted in a distortion of the threefold image of the human being into a dualism of body and soul causing a restriction of the spiritual freedom of humanity. Therefore the year 869 can be regarded as a turning point in the development of European cultural life. It is the cultural task of Waldorf schools to restore the threefold picture of humanity in a practical manner.

The 9th century began with the coronation of the Frankish king Charlemagne as Emperor Carolus Magnus. With this deed Pope Leo III laid the foundation for the event of 869. By the coronation of Charlemagne spiritual life in Western Europe was placed under the authority of the pope in Rome. Until that moment the ever-growing Frankish realm stood in a free relationship to the Church in Rome. Evolving Christianity in Frankish territory had always been dominated by the influence of the Irish-Celtic spirit. Also in Charlemagne's court school the Irish, as well as Anglo-Saxons with an Irish orientation, were always welcome.

Even the great teacher Alcuin of York can be placed partly in this stream, as can Waldo von Reichenau and Hugo of Tours.[4]

Among the first teachers in the first Waldorf school, Herbert Hahn and Walter Johannes Stein felt themselves related to these personages from Carolingian times.[5] When Alcuin, who was the leader of the court school of Charlemagne, died in 804, the influence of the priests and teachers who were Rome-oriented grew progressively stronger. Charlemagne's biographer Einhard played an important role in this process. In his *Vita Caroli Magni (Life of Charlemagne)* he systematically omitted the names of those teachers who worked more in the Irish-Celtic spirit.[6] Within the Rome-oriented stream the principle of organization became more and more important, while the Irish-Celtic stream wanted to preserve the spiritual autonomy of the individual. The latter stream attached utmost importance to this spiritual autonomy, while the former placed itself under the authority of the pope in Rome, also in spiritual respects.

It is important to compare the situation of that time with the current problems in Waldorf schools. Today also we have the question of the spiritual autonomy of the teacher in relation to the standards established by the state. This comparison need not create a polarity if we realize that both in the 9th century and now these streams each have their value and significance. Only when one stream tries to dominate the other does it become a problem. The following passage of the New Testament is applicable here: "When two are gathered in my name, I am in the midst of them."

As we have seen, in the 9th century it was difficult to give form to this middle position for cooperation in an impulse for educational renewal at the Carolingian court school. That the relationship between this school and Waldorf schools is not just conjecture is confirmed by a remark Steiner made to Walter Johannes Stein: "The teachers were Aristotelians and the students Saxons from the days of Charlemagne."[7]

In other indications Steiner also confirms the relationship between the foundation of the first Waldorf school and the teachers around Charlemagne. For instance, it apparently happened regularly to Emil Molt that the children on the playground were unkind to him. In his perplexity he asked advice from Steiner who replied with words somewhat as follows: "What do you want? In a prior life they were the Saxons whom you as Charlemagne fought against all the time, who were killed." (Source: H.H. Schöffler)

For anyone who is not familiar with the difficulties between Charlemagne and the Saxons,* these words will not have the significance they may have had for Emil Molt. Here Steiner used what was happening to a long-time, dedicated spiritual pupil through his involvement with the Waldorf school to bring him to karmic insight in a way that left him completely free.[8] Whether Emil Molt indeed lived in full realization of a karmic connection with Charlemagne is something I cannot confirm. And yet for a number of pioneer teachers of the school in Stuttgart, this was a reality they could experience.

These examples can lead to the conviction that the karmic relationship of the Carolingian court school with the foundation of the Waldorf school was for Steiner a spiritual reality. We should note, however, that he apparently did not proclaim this openly, but he tried to awaken the individuals involved to a consciousness of their karma.

Thus, around Charlemagne a struggle took place for the leadership of the educational impulse that was to give form to cultural life in Europe into the late Middle Ages. In outer respects, the Irish lost this struggle. Thanks to Steiner we know that after its outer defeat this Irish-Celtic stream continued to work in a hidden way as the stream of Grail Christianity.[9] Outer cultural development was now controlled by Rome. By his unexpected coronation as Emperor, Charlemagne was the one who helped seal this destiny. He carries part of the guilt for a development that would lead to the denial of the threefold nature of the human being in 869. (Opinions about the coronation remain divided. The general view is that Charlemagne realized what the pope had in mind only when he felt the crown put on his head.)

Out of this karmic debt which, by the way, did not have its origin in a conscious decision, the will was born in Emil Molt, who was the owner/manager of a factory, to lay the seed for a cultural impulse that would lead to the restoration of the true human image: spirit, soul and body. In his weighty destiny moments Charlemagne never stood alone. He was always carried and supported by the spiritual world. There is a statement by Steiner that clarifies this: "Charlemagne, who came from the East—he was a reincarnation of a lofty Indian adept—was an instrument of the spiritual individuality symbolized by the name Titurel."[10]

---

* Note: Charlemagne fought many wars against the Saxons in his realm because they kept rebelling against his rule. [Trans.]

As most Waldorf teachers know from the familiar Grail stories, Titurel was the founder of the Grail family and the builder of the Grail Temple. Is it not a deeply touching movement of destiny that in an outer sense Charlemagne connected himself with the Roman influence which would lead to 'abolishing the spirit' while in an inner sense he was completely permeated by the being of Titurel? It is as if Titurel knew that for a certain period of time it would be a historical necessity for knowledge of the spirit to be lost in Europe. In this regard a statement by Steiner in the same session dovetails with this: "One can have historical and moral views of a historical personality that often differ greatly from the views a clairvoyant obtains through his or her experiences. In any case, Charlemagne was destined to advance evolution in a certain way."[11]

Because from the year 800 on the authority of the pope was becoming more and more important in the Frankish realm, the decisions of the Councils had a steadily growing significance for cultural life in western and central Europe. That was the reason why the decision of the Council of 869 had such heavy and long-lasting consequences. Through our professional karma and perhaps also through our personal destiny, we stand as Waldorf teachers in the midst of the consequences of this cultural problem. That realization may be depressing if it is only half conscious. I see a challenge here to squarely face the problem consciously, and to draw out of this the courage and enthusiasm to fulfill our pedagogical task in a culture-renewing manner. I see the current problems within the Waldorf school movement in relation to the karmic situations discussed here. Viewed from the perspective of its karma from the 9th century, for the Waldorf school movement the restoration of the threefold image of the human being is a significant and magnificent task. I hope that this chapter can make a contribution to enthusiasm for the pedagogical impulse out of the search for the karma of the Waldorf school movement.

3

The Significance of the Educational Impulse of Charlemagne

$\mathcal{T}$he educational impulse of Charlemagne is connected with a great change in the human being that was taking place in the 9th century. Rudolf Steiner describes this process and indicates that since the 4th century the spiritual development of European humanity was guided more and more by a different hierarchy of spiritual beings than before.

Steiner shows this by calling attention to the change that was occurring in human thinking: The rulership of thinking in its original, cosmic quality was being transferred by the hierarchy of the Spirits of Form (Exusiai) to the Spirits of Personality (Archai). This was important because the manner in which the Spirits of Form bring cosmic thinking into relation with the human being is totally different from the way the Spirits of Personality do this.

> The Spirits of Form drew these thoughts out of the cosmic reservoir of thoughts in order to instill them into human beings from outside. The human being took the cosmic thoughts into himself and willy-nilly felt like a creature propelled forward in the floods and waves produced in the cosmos by the Spirits of Form. The world of thoughts within the cosmos transmitted its harmony to humanity itself. But humanity was unfree in the cosmos! Today the human being has acquired the freedom to work out his own thoughts, but these thoughts would all remain hermits in the cosmos if they have not been taken from and brought back again into the cosmic harmony. And in our epoch this comes to pass through the Archai.[12]

In the same lecture, Steiner indicates that this transfer from the Spirits of Form to the Spirits of Personality was a long process that extended from the 4th to the 15th century. From other statements it appears that this process comes to a first stage of completion in the 9th century. In late lectures of 1924, Steiner spoke several times about the 9th century as the time when the cosmic intelligence was placed within the reach of the increasingly independent human being.

Charlemagne wanted to place his educational impulse in the service of this emerging freedom of thinking. One of the consequences of this was that he came into conflict with the peoples who wanted to preserve thinking as a gift bestowed on them from the outside by the Spirits of Form. Thus erupted the long battle with the Saxons in the east who wanted to remain true to Odin's wisdom in their thinking. They experienced this wisdom as a gift from the gods, coming to them from the outside, and thus behind the Odin wisdom of the Saxons we may sense the still continuing influence of the Spirits of Form.

The war with the Saxons really flared up in 772 when Charlemagne undertook a campaign to the Externsteine, the principal sanctuary of the German tribes, and had the Irminsul (Irmin column) cut down. This was a tall column that formed the connection between the earth and Asgard, the realm of the gods. Steiner has confirmed that the center of the activity of the Asen was located in the spiritual world above the Externsteine.[13]

In the south too Charlemagne battled a people who wanted to remain true to the influence of the Spirits of Form in their thinking, namely the Saracens who occupied Spain in the 9th century. A kind of mingling of Christianity and Islam took place in Spain. Although there was great cultural and religious freedom in the large cities such as Barcelona, Granada and Toledo, this was inspired from an Islamic spiritual life that accepted Allah as the only god.

In the experience of Jews and Muslims, Allah has a relationship with Yahweh from the Old Testament. Yahweh is one of the Elohim; Genesis speaks of Yahweh-Elohim. And the Elohim are Spirits of Form, Exusiai. The cult of Yahweh or Allah as the only god gives the human life of thinking the characteristic that it makes itself dependent on the hierarchy of the Spirits of Form. For this reason the conviction lives in Islam that human thinking does not possess any lasting independence. In this view, thinking fell into a state of improper independence because of the physical sheath, which was a consequence of the fall into sin. After death this thinking is absorbed again into the 'ocean' of divine thinking. This conviction is inspired by the influence of the Spirits of Form that could still be felt in the 9th century.

During the time when Charlemagne fought his battles with the Saxons, an embassy from Spain came to him to invoke his help against the Muslims. Charles decided to march across the Pyrenees with his army. But this campaign was not to have a good outcome for the Frankish king since the inhabitants of the area around Barcelona did not feel threatened by the Muslims, and therefore did not join his invading force. This was the reason why he decided to go back to France. But in a mountain pass near Ronceval, the rear guard of his army was unexpectedly attacked, and Roland, one of the king's most beloved generals, was killed.

These wars in east and south represented in actuality a spiritual battle the significance of which has to do with the question of whether human thinking would become free or not. The leading influence of the Spirits of Form had to cede place to a relationship forged by the human being himself with the Spirits of Personality. The educational impulse that emanated from the school at the Carolingian court stood in service of this new development in thinking.

In this regard also, we can see a parallel with Waldorf pedagogy in our century. Right at the beginning of the Waldorf school in Stuttgart, Steiner pointed out that it was the task of Waldorf education to protect human intelligence from hardening, which would lead to a progressively closer connection of this intelligence with amoral, lying and evil forces.[14]

This is a problem with which Waldorf schools have to cope today. It is the consequence of the development that took place in relation to thinking between the 4th and 15th centuries. Because our thinking is no longer directly ruled by spiritual beings, Ahrimanic beings have the possibility to ensconce themselves in this life of thought. In a certain sense, therefore, Charlemagne waged a spiritual battle to save human thinking through his educational impulse. As was mentioned before, the spiritual power of the Grail King Titurel worked in Charlemagne. Titurel bestowed on him the inspiration to form spiritual life in Europe in such a way that human thinking could find its own free relationship with the Spirits of Personality. Together with Alcuin, the leader of the court school, Charlemagne tried to develop a curriculum on the basis of the Seven Liberal Arts that date back to Greek times. In a similar way, it was Karl Stockmeyer who, at the request of Emil Molt and Rudolf Steiner, gave the curriculum of the Waldorf school form in such a way that it could be shown to the state authorities.

In the 9th century the program of the Seven Liberal Arts was an appropriate curriculum and educational form to give human intelligence, while it was freeing itself from spiritual dominance, the possibility of making a connection with the Spirits of Personality. In the following we will describe the Carolingian curriculum of the Seven Liberal Arts as developed by Alcuin in Aachen and Tours from this point of view.

For Alcuin, the leader and founder of the court school of Charlemagne, the method of the Seven Liberal Arts was of particular educational value, both for young people who were to receive a spiritual task as priests and for those who expected to take on secular duties as members of the nobility. Alcuin's principal goal in the study of the Seven Liberal Arts was for the pupil to attain to virtuous wisdom through the discipline of a step-by-step, rigorous practice of science. He describes this very clearly in his important work *Disputatio de Vera Philosophia (Debate about True Philosophy)*. From the following passage of this work we can witness how real and alive the spirit, and also the connection with angels, was still experienced by the 9th century human being.

The Way of Wisdom Is Not an Outward Path but an Inward One

The human being is a living being equipped with a spirit. This is the better part of himself that is immortal and an image of his creator. For this reason, everything he strives for outside himself, such as wealth, is foreign to his essence, while all he develops in himself, such as wisdom, is part of his essence. Only the wise person deals rightly with earthly goods. And it is wisdom which lifts up the lowly and raises the poor out of the dust so they can take their place, together with the prince, on the throne of glory.

The Laborious Path Toward Wisdom

The ornament of wisdom can be conquered only through effort. Just as fighting is part of a soldier's life, and physical effort part of that of a peasant, it is said of the practice of science that its roots are bitter but its fruits sweet. Even more diligently than Plato do pupils have to follow their teacher, because he not only leads them on the way of the Seven Liberal Arts, but also to that wisdom that opens the door to eternal life. For this, however, divine grace is needed. … Education has to lead step by step from below above. Thus the feathers of virtue will gradually grow with which, in the end, the pupil can reach the pure heights of the ether where he can enter the storerooms of God. In the worthy conduct of the teacher and in the truth of his words, the confidence of the pupil will grow that from his earliest youth, by contemplating things in beauty, he has climbed the stairway to wisdom. For thoughts are not only nourishment for gods and angels, but they are also ornaments for the soul.

The House of Wisdom

Solomon said that wisdom built a house resting on seven pillars. This sentence can be applied to Christ himself, who built up his physicality in the body of Mary and was supported in this by the seven gifts of the Holy Spirit. This saying can also relate to the Church as the House of God. By divine wisdom the Church has been endowed with these seven gifts. But still, in every conceivable situation wisdom is sustained by the seven pillars of the Liberal Arts. The only way to come to complete science is by raising oneself to wisdom by raising oneself on these seven steps, or pillars. This path ascending the seven steps of Philosophia is the one we shall take. Divine grace is not only a condition for going this way, but is also necessary as companion and guide on this path of learning.

This is a very clear exposition from Alcuin's writing about the goal of education in the Seven Liberal Arts. Alcuin describes the intimate relationship between the Seven Liberal Arts and divine wisdom. The way up the seven steps is inextricably connected with Wisdom as divine Grace. He also speaks of the path of learning as a path of seven steps or pillars of Philosophia. In Greek Wisdom is called Sophia. The path of learning of the Seven Liberal Arts is taken by those who are friends (*philoi*) of Wisdom: Philo-Sophia. Wisdom is also connected with the seven gifts of the Holy Spirit. Divine Grace meets teacher and pupil in the practice of the Seven Liberal Arts.

In addition, Alcuin describes the Seven Liberal Arts as the pillars of the house of Wisdom. Alcuin lives with the principle of the temple of Solomon. His view of the path of learning as the pillars of the temple gives a picture we can make for ourselves of his teaching an important quality.

In our Waldorf curriculum many elements of this path through the Seven Liberal Arts can be recognized. Both then and now it is the striving to awaken the human being in his individual spiritual strength, without breaking the connection with the spiritual world in the process.

4

Knight Roland, Charlemagne's Favorite Paladin

On the eve of the campaign against the Saxons in the year 772, Charlemagne and his retinue were staying on his estate in the (now Dutch) town of Nijmegen. Charles liked it there, but this time it was an exceptional pleasure because Roland, his favorite paladin, was to get married. The feast was especially splendid because of the presence of a large number of noblemen. They were there to accompany Charles and help him inflict a final defeat on the Saxons and other Germanic tribes led by Duke Widukind on their own turf on the other side of the Rhine. Roland would be among them.

One of Charlemagne's counselors, Waldo von Reichenau, was considering the possibility of making yet another effort to awaken comprehension of the mystery of Christianity with the Germanic priests. His penchant for Irish-Celtic Christianity inspired him to make Charles more and more enthusiastic for the old songs from the Edda. The memory of Wotan, Thor, Widar and Iduna must not be lost, and even the doubtful veneration of Freya had its origin in the worship of the pure eternal feminine.

But Charles knew that after Roland's wedding the decisive battle would be fought, and that the destruction of the Irminsul at the enigmatic Externsteine[15] would be inevitable. Charles also knew that this deed would kindle the hatred of the Saxons, and especially of their Duke Widukind, into a blazing fire, but he was convinced that the spirit of the time demanded the lasting Christianization of the Germanic peoples. Discussion and understanding had been fruitless in his view. Now the time had come to commit an inexorable and irreversible deed: The path to Asgard would be cut off by the destruction of the Irminsul. The result would be that the Germanic priests would lose their clairvoyance.

Charles had also decided not to leave the vanquished people to their own lot, but to found schools in which these people, who carried a strong consciousness of self, could practice free thinking. In reading and writing they would be allowed to continue to use their own language besides Latin. Their own sagas and legends could be used as teaching and practice material along with Roman and Greek literature.

The event in the spring of 772 seems to find its continuation on September 7, 1919. On that day too a wedding was celebrated. And in the house of the cigarette manufacturer Emil Molt again a group of people had assembled, ready for battle. Earlier in the day Steiner had pointed out to them the seriousness of their intentions. On behalf of the good spirits who work for the welfare of humanity, he gave special thanks to Emil Molt for his courageous striving that had led to the founding of the first Waldorf school. Then Steiner went to each of the twelve future teachers, looked them earnestly in the eye and shook their hand.

This event took place in the worthy setting of a room in which the table and chairs were swathed in deep blue. Before the beginning of the meal, Emil Molt had perhaps been sitting in his study to prepare the speech he was to give. Then we would have seen him at his desk in the same blue atmosphere there had been at the school opening that morning. His study was also deep blue. Why? Charlemagne's coat of arms had a deep blue field. It is as if already in the color, which clothed the decisive moments of this day, the connection with the Carolingian school movement could be experienced.

The wedding was festive. Paul Baumann, who would become the first music teacher at the Waldorf school, married Elisabeth Dollfus, the first eurythmist at the school. The wedding was a wondrous musical expression for the intentions that lived in the souls of the entire teachers' community around Emil Molt, and of which Steiner said that the founding of the Waldorf school was a "festive act of the world order." The same day, at the opening of the school itself, Paul Baumann started the proceedings by taking place behind the grand piano in the city auditorium and presenting the Prelude in C-sharp from Johann Sebastian Bach's *Well-Tempered Clavier.*

Paul Baumann

During the time the school was being created, Paul Baumann proved to be a 'martial' man, ready for battle. This was expressed by his colleague Herbert Hahn who had first met him as a fiery speaker for the impulse of social threefolding.

Elisabeth Baumann

Herbert Hahn described his impression of Paul Baumann in striking words: "Among the first twelve teachers who belonged to the College of the Waldorf school, Paul Baumann was one of the most remarkable. I experienced him for the first time when he acted as moderator in a discussion on social threefolding, the movement that preceded the creation of the Waldorf school. He did not speak for a long time, but what he said was clear, sharp, and hit the mark. As he stepped back from the podium I felt: 'He is like a knight who comes charging in on a somewhat obnoxious horse and with a drawn sword. It was as if you could still hear the swishing of the sword through the air…' "[16]

This is a striking way to characterize Paul Baumann. It is as if Herbert Hahn described an experience here that shows a relationship with the results that can arise from the karma exercises Steiner gave in order to achieve insight into prior lives of people who in certain events make a deep impression on us. In addition, the description also speaks of a certain consciousness of chivalry as a characteristic—for this human being.

In 1933 Paul Baumann became the leader of the school, when the state demanded that the school create this position. He undertook this because his colleagues gave him their trust in this task.

Two years later he made a trip to Spain and Morocco where he experienced the encounter with Spanish and Moorish culture with great intensity. His daughter Christine Baumann said that "on this trip the deeper layers of his being had been touched." He experienced this southern world as a colorful, light, enigmatic memory of childhood, and he moved into it in a kind of meditative, attentive mood. Another two years later, in 1937, Paul and his family left Germany. In 1938 the school was closed by the Nazis.

Now let us go back to Charlemagne's paladin, Roland, and see what happened to him. After the wedding, Charlemagne and his army did indeed invade the land of the Saxons and cut down the Irminsul. The war was to last for many more years. Then a Reichstag[17] took place, for the first time on Saxon territory. Representatives from all parts of the empire came together in Paderborn. Even the ousted Caliph of Baghdad, Suleiman, appeared, and this man was able to convince Charlemagne to undertake a campaign against his opponent Abdul-Rahman in Spain.

In 778 Charlemagne assembled a large army for this venture. But great was his disappointment when he found out that the local Christians felt no need for any assistance from Charlemagne and his Frankish knights. They were living in harmony with the Muslims and did not want war. It turned out that Suleiman had just wanted to use Charlemagne for his own purposes. Charles then decided to go back. The retreat went well until near Ronceval he heard horn sounds from the rear

From a 14th century manuscript,
'Les Grandes Chroniques de France'

guard. It was the horn 'Oliphant,' Roland's horn whose mighty sounds echoed in the mountains. Charlemagne immediately turned around with the advance party to come to the aid of the rear guard that was commanded by Roland. But it was too late; the entire rear guard had been ambushed and slaughtered in an unequal battle. Roland was found with 'Oliphant' by his side and his legendary sword hidden under his body. Charles was inconsolable because of the loss of this knight whom he had loved as his own son.

In Paul Baumann, the first music teacher of the Waldorf school, we can bring the characteristics of this battle-ready knight to life again. And the wedding that was celebrated in Nijmegen at Easter time in 772 goes, on a completely different level, through a kind of resurrection around Michaelmas 1919. Paul Baumann fought in a musical-martial way for the Waldorf school impulse!

In the 8th century, the time when Charlemagne founded his schools, the archangel Raphael was the reigning time spirit. In the cycle of the year, it is Eastertime when Raphael's healing influence is at its peak. In the 20th century the archangel Michael is the active time spirit. In the Waldorf schools this is, every year again, the first festival we celebrate with the children.

5

EMIL MOLT AND HERMANN HESSE

*T*he year when Rudolf Steiner first spoke in public about the threefold nature of the human being, which would become the basis for the movement toward the threefold social order and the Waldorf school movement, Emil Molt found his old school friend Hermann Hesse again. Emil Molt relates the following about this encounter: "During the [First World] War I ran into a former buddy from my school years in Calw. This was Hermann Hesse. It happened as follows: When the war of the trenches had come to a deadlock, it became clear to me that the soldiers not only needed tobacco but also spiritual nourishment. Giving them cigarettes no longer seemed sufficient to me. Encouraged by a conversation with the editor of the periodical *Lese (Read)*, I had the idea to publish good literature in little books so they could easily be stuffed in the cigarette cartons.

"From this a second plan was born, namely to do something for the Swabian poets who were having a very hard time during the war. On behalf of my company, I invited Hermann Hesse to participate in this project. In a friendly letter he agreed to do this and then added: 'Your letter is signed E. Molt; if this is my old school friend from Calw, I request that you convey my greetings to him.' Soon after that he visited Stuttgart. He lived at that time in the old Welti house in Bern (Switzerland) after he had left Gaiënhofen. For twenty years we had not had any personal contact, but this did not prevent our reunion from being joyful. A new friendship developed between us which deepened from year to year. Today, after another twenty years, I might be inclined to write down the history of my friendship with Hesse."

In Herman Hesse, Emil Molt found a partner in his initiative to bring the soldiers in the field in contact with literature and also with a number of Steiner's writings, such as the *Calendar of the Soul* and the fairy tales from the mystery dramas. Hermann Hesse also made it possible for the prisoners of war to receive little books with weekly verses and Steiner's lecture "Philosophy and

Anthroposophy." During this time Hermann Hesse wrote a poem he dedicated to Emil and Berta Molt, which illustrates his deep connection with them.

Im vierten Kriegsjahr

Wenn auch der Abend kalt und traurig ist
Und Regen rauscht
Ich singe doch mein Lied zu dieser Frist
Weiss nicht, wer lauscht.
Wenn auch die Welt in Krieg und Angst erstickt
An manchem Ort
Brennt Heimlich doch, ob niemand sie erblickt
Die Liebe fort.

In the Fourth Year of War

Although the evening is cold and dreary
And rain rushes down,
Yet I sing my song at the usual time.
Although the world is strangled in war and fear
Who knows who listens?
In many a place
Yet secretly, though no one sees,
Love burns forth.*

Although the world is strangled in war and fear, in the same year that Emil Molt took the first step toward the founding of the first Waldorf school, Hermann Hesse became known all over the world because of his pedagogical novel *Demian*.

The renewal of the friendship between Emil Molt and Hermann Hesse took place in 1917. During that year Hesse spent some of the winter months with the Molts in St. Moritz, Switzerland. The conversations about their shared youth in Calw, as well as the ski trips they made in the Swiss mountains, confirmed the renewed friendship.

Hermann Hesse

---

* Note: My translation – P.M.

As we mentioned before, it was in 1917 that Steiner brought out his view of the threefold nature of the human being, which became the starting point for the first Waldorf school and the Waldorf impulse as a world movement. In the years after 1919, the year the school was founded, Hermann Hesse remained a welcome guest in the house of the Molt family. This was the house where, on the day the school was opened, Steiner and the first twelve teachers were treated to a festive meal. (This festive meal also celebrated the marriage of Paul Baumann and Elisabeth Dolfus, both teachers at the Waldorf school.) Steiner was to come here often in subsequent years.

Although Hermann Hesse came very close to Steiner via his friendship with Emil Molt, he still rejected him. Emil Molt wrote the following about this:

> It was painful for us that Hermann Hesse was not able to appreciate our world view. And yet he knew several of Steiner's books and read from time to time in *Knowledge of Higher Worlds*. But earlier he had been an Indian-oriented theosophist. This probably prevented him from finding a right relationship to the activity of thinking. Fichte and Hegel worked on him like a red flag on a bull. Basically he saw in all the various religions one and the same thing. For him Buddha, Lao-Tse (who was one of his favorites), Zarathustra and Jesus were all equivalent leaders of humanity. He had no feeling for possible differentiation and development of religious conceptions.

And then follows an important sentence:

> His being [Hermann Hesse] was split: On the one hand he was deeply Christian [his father and grandfather had been dedicated missionaries], but on the other hand he had a strong interest in the East, the Indian stream.

Thus Emil Molt recognized in Hesse a deep Christian but also an Indian side, which together formed a split in his personality that caused him to lack confidence in thinking. And it is exactly this confidence in thinking as the bridge to the spiritual world which is the basis of anthroposophy as founded by Rudolf Steiner. If Christianity is not penetrated by thinking, it remains belief and rigidifies into dogmas.

In Carolingian times the Roman Catholic Church chose this latter way. Pope Nicolas I made the weighty decision in the 9th century to promote a dogmatic Christianity out of Rome in European spiritual life. This decision was prepared in Carolingian times around the turn of the 8th to the 9th century. Among the Christian leaders around Charlemagne a struggle took place either for a religion that was free in its research and expression—as represented by the Irish-Celtic teachers such as Waldo von Reichenau—or for following dogmatic Rome as represented by Einhard.

Now, we see in Charlemagne's most intimate inner circle a scholar and priest who, as an Anglo-Saxon from York (England), had had direct experience of the Irish-Celtic spirit. This explains why he again and again wanted to make a place for the Seven Liberal Arts in the Carolingian schools. Nevertheless, he also unconditionally accepted the primacy of Rome, both in regard to dogmatic faith and ecclesiastical politics. This was Alcuin. Charlemagne met him in Parma, Italy. They were both at the height of their capacities, Alcuin as scholar and poet-author, Charlemagne as enterprising statesman.

Charlemagne was immediately impressed by Alcuin and proposed that he become his counselor with a twofold task. One was to give form to education in the realm of the Franks; the other to be Charlemagne's advisor in ecclesiastical politics. Alcuin agreed to this and thus began their collaboration. In education he respected the literary element that lived in the people. This led to the creation of a collection of stories around Odin. At the college level Alcuin stimulated the practice of the Seven Liberal Arts. There exists a complete course in logic Alcuin wrote in the form of a dialog between himself and Charlemagne. In addition, however, he connected Charlemagne in political and ecclesiastical respects with Rome. Alcuin's former activity may have been rooted in non-dogmatic, esoteric Christianity, but his later work gave support to exoteric Christianity that emanated from Rome. Walter Johannes Stein sees the coronation of Charlemagne as Emperor at Christmas 800 in Rome as the definitive connection between esoteric and exoteric Christianity. Alcuin worked toward this connection, and in his day this was justified and timely.

In our time the esoteric element has to become directly active again in the world. Not for nothing did Steiner call the Waldorf school movement the model of anthroposophy as esotericism working fruitfully in the world. Emil Molt stood fully in this impulse. Part of the being of Hermann Hesse participated in it through Emil Molt as an expression of old karma. But did not Hermann Hesse's rejection of anthroposophy bear fruit for the Waldorf school movement in a certain sense? Did not Hesse's books create a transition phase for many who were looking to become teachers or parents at the Waldorf school?

In the 1970s the Waldorf school movement experienced explosive growth. Just preceding this we see the growth of the youth movement of the late 1960s and early 1970s. Confidence in Western science disappeared among youth. Universities were occupied and anti-science slogans sounded in the streets of Paris. In this revolution confidence in thinking was in danger of being lost. Indian gurus gratefully took advantage of this. And exactly at this time the work of Hermann Hesse was rediscovered in America. Gradually also in Europe there was no student at European universities and schools who had not read his work. His work encompasses both East and West, but it always stands on the world of thinking of a Middle-European human being. The autonomy and uniqueness of the human individuality runs through his work like a red thread. He attempts to bridge duality.

Hesse leads the reader to the boundary, and there he stops. The same is true for his search for a new spiritual science and a new school system in his book *The Glass Bead Game*; he leaves the reader standing at the point where he is expected to take up his own striving—to think.

Thus Hermann Hesse became for a number of young people who were searching for a spiritual science that is Christian and can have an effect in the culture, a messenger, a portal to a meeting with Emil Molt in the Waldorf school and, with him, the great spiritual teacher Rudolf Steiner. With the latter they were able to start the real work, while Hermann Hesse remained silently behind. But who knows … he may be smiling!

Hermann Hesse hiking in Switzerland

6

ALCUIN, LEADER OF THE COURT SCHOOL OF CHARLEMAGNE, AND KARL STOCKMEYER

*I*n the course of my research into the figure of Alcuin, a parallel arose for me, not only in relation to his educational impulse, but also in his entire biography, with the leader (coordinator) of the first Waldorf school in Stuttgart, E.A. Karl Stockmeyer. It is not my intention to make this look like a karmic relationship, although I would certainly not exclude that as a possibility. Rather I want to try to let the important facts in the biographies of these two men speak for themselves. Let's first take a look at Karl Stockmeyer's biography.

E.A. Karl Stockmeyer was born in Karlsruhe on June 7, 1886, the son of the artist Karl W.H. Stockmeyer. He went to school in Malsch and in Detmolt, a little town in the immediate vicinity of the Externsteine. From 1898 he went to school in Karlsruhe, together with his two sisters. The daily trek from their home through a forest to the city took many hours. During the winter of 1890 the family lived in the vicinity of Naples where his father had to create a large painting. When after the turn of the century Karl's final exams were approaching, he went to Karlsruhe to live with a local family and prepare thoroughly for the exams. This couple had a connection with the Theosophical Society. Through them Karl attended a lecture by Rudolf Steiner on November 25, 1904, which would prove to be of critical significance for this scientifically-thinking nineteen-year-old.

The year after, he met Steiner for a second time. Steiner then discussed the latest mathematical theories with him. At that time Karl began to study *The Philosophy of Freedom*, the book he would work with for the rest of his life. In the fall of 1905 Karl and his older sister entered the University of Heidelberg where he also wanted to join the local theosophical lodge; however, this was impossible because he was not yet twenty-one. But he was able to attend Steiner's lectures.

31

Finally in 1907 the day came that he was accepted as member of the Theosophical Society and he immediately participated in the Congress in Munich, together with his parents and sisters. Karl was deeply impressed by the way Steiner had transformed the auditorium. Especially the image of the painted columns along the walls stayed with him the entire following year. In the fall of the same year Karl became a member of the Esoteric School, and thus Steiner became his guide on the path of spiritual development. "I tried to represent spiritual-

E.A. Karl Stockmeyer

scientific insights to myself in such a way that it became possible to place them in the spiritual space of the *Philosophy of Freedom.*" This clearly demonstrates that Karl wanted to avoid passive thinking, and he remained an original thinker within the Theosophical Society. In his relationship with Steiner he made an impression of independence and of an orientation toward investigation and research.

All winter Karl worked with the themes of the columns he had so intensely observed in Munich. He tried painting, drawing and clay to take in this language of form as livingly as possible. In the spring of 1908 he showed his work to Steiner and asked him the question that, as a kind of Parsifal question, came to fruition in the building of the first Goetheanum. The question was what architecture would belong to the columns. Steiner replied that the seven columns, arranged in two east-west directed rows, enclose an elliptical space. He also indicated how the roof could be designed in the form of a dome. Karl's father proved to be an enthusiastic supporter of the idea of a building project in the immediate vicinity of his house.

Although the ultimate fruits of this model in Malsch (the crypt of the house of the Society in Stuttgart and the first Goetheanum) have not survived, the model itself, a small temple, can still be visited on the grounds of the social-therapeutic institute that was established in the family home of the Stockmeyers. It is no exaggeration when we say that this building impulse of Karl Stockmeyer can be regarded as the beginning of a new type of temple construction in service of the modern Christian mysteries.

During his studies in Heidelberg, which had a broad orientation, architecture became more and more important. When around Easter 1909 the full moon was shining, Steiner came to Malsch to lay the foundation stone of this partly underground temple. In the same year Karl decided to become a teacher, a profession for which he received his credentials two years later. While he was getting his first teaching experience in Magdeburg, he also made the calculations for the complicated domed vaulted roof of the house of the Anthroposophical Society in Stuttgart. Then he became math and physics teacher at a public school in Karlsruhe. After the outbreak of World War I, he taught at a teachers training center. All this time he remained a faithful student of both spiritual science and philosophy. During the war he occupied himself especially with Hegel.

Alcuin was born between 730 and 735 in or close to York in northeast England. He was related to Willibrord, the archbishop of the Frisians, who died in 739, and whose biography he would later write. When Alcuin was taken to the cathedral school as a young boy, he became Archbishop Egbert's favorite student.

When he was around nine years old, the cathedral and monastery burned to the ground on Sunday April 23, 741. With this event the boy, who was then at an age when a child no longer experiences the world around him as self-evident, saw the famous and familiar temple of Christianity consumed by flames. It must have been a great shock for him that he never forgot. Remembering that 8th century churches were largely made of wood, we can only imagine the extent of the fire by comparing it with that of the fire of the first Goetheanum on New Year's Eve in 1922. In York the columns must also have stood there burning like torches long after the roof had caved in. Alcuin had to experience how the 'house of wisdom' perished in the fire. When we connect this biographical fact with the words he wrote in his *Disputatio de Vera Philosophia* (see chapter 3), we can experience how this fire and the subsequent building impulse of the House of Wisdom run through Alcuin's biography as a red thread.

After this event we hear, besides about Egbert, about Aelbert, a priest and nobleman, as Alcuin's principal teacher. Alcuin wrote about his lessons: "He opened out the mysteries of Holy Scripture and gave us a look into the abyss of law ancient and unfulfilled." In a letter in which Alcuin described his insights into the zodiac and its astronomical laws, he said the following about Aelbert: "My master very often said to me: 'They were the wisest men who discerned these arts in Nature. It is a great disgrace for us to let them die out in our time.' " The moments Aelbert was able to escape from his work in church and classroom were spent in his beloved library. Alcuin left us a catalog of this enormous library which contained works from both the teachers of antiquity and the church fathers.

Aelbert took Alcuin with him on his first journey to Continental Europe. They visited Pavia and Rome, and attended a discussion between a Jewish scholar and Peter of Pisa. They also stopped at the monastery of the Etichones (connected with St. Odile of Alsace) in Murbach. Later Alcuin wrote about this: "Once I came with my master to your community and saw and loved its excellent way of life—so much that I longed to be there as one of you." For Alcuin, Aelbert was the great teacher who introduced him in a scientific manner to the secrets of both antiquity and Christianity, while at the same time bringing him into the world. For the rest of his life Alcuin spoke about his teacher with the greatest reverence as 'father and brother and most honored friend.'

After Egbert's death Aelbert succeeded him as archbishop of York. One of his first deeds was to make sure that the cathedral, which had been lying in ruins for twenty-five years, would be rebuilt. He gave this work to the then thirty-three-year-old Alcuin as his task. Together with another ex-pupil of Aelbert, Eanbald, Alcuin did a marvelous job. The House of Wisdom was rebuilt, but now with massive stone columns, and with many side chapels with some thirty altars. During this entire work Alcuin also carried the responsibility for the educational program at the cathedral school which was famous even on the Continent at that time.

In these descriptions of Alcuin's and Stockmeyer's youths we can experience striking similarities, for instance in relation to temple building, in which the motif of seven pillars is of central importance. Both of them worked as teachers and at the same time as builders. Alcuin saw the predecessor building of his cathedral going up in flames while Stockmeyer had to experience the destruction of the first Goetheanum by fire. There is a charcoal drawing of the burning Goetheanum made after the roof had already caved in showing the columns, which had been formed by Karl and his father in wood for the first time in history, burning in the midst of the fire and reaching up as torches into the sky. At that time, 1922, Stockmeyer had already been working full-time with Emil Molt for three years as teacher and also as the person responsible for contact with the government authorities in order to make this totally new form of education at the Waldorf school in Stuttgart possible.

Karl was thirty-three years old when he put himself fully in service of the Waldorf school impulse. Alcuin was also thirty-three when Aelbert gave him the leadership of the cathedral school and, in addition, the task of rebuilding the cathedral. Just as Stockmeyer gained his own building and education experience before he joined Emil Molt for the founding of the Waldorf school in 1919, similarly Alcuin gained his own experience in building and education before he went to Aachen to take on the leadership of the Carolingian court school in 782. At the court school Charlemagne tried to gather the best teachers of his empire.

The following anecdote illustrates this. One day Alcuin was speaking about the lives of St. Augustine and St. Jerome. The king exclaimed almost in despair: "I wish I had just twelve of such people in my realm." Alcuin then reprimanded him: "The Lord our God had only two such men, and you want twelve of them?"[18] And yet, this striving of Charlemagne for the number twelve was not just hubris; it shows how strongly the spiritual laws underlying the forming of Christian community were living in him. In his reprimand, Alcuin himself pointed to the circle of apostles, the archetype from which the twelve Knights of the Round Table derived their form. The Irish and Anglo-Saxon monks also came to the continent of Europe in groups of twelve. In the number twelve it is possible to unite all karmic directions of human striving, and thus it provides the broadest possible foundation for a community. Alcuin saw the intention of Charlemagne as unachievable. And it is exactly this unfulfilled striving for a community of twelve that was realized by Stockmeyer in the formation of the first community of Waldorf school teachers.

To conclude this chapter I would like to quote a description by Johannes Tautz of the early days of the first Waldorf school. "Late May conversations took place with Steiner about the formation of a group of teachers for the school that was being founded. Stockmeyer was advised to start traveling around like a theater director who is looking for talent to put together an ensemble." On July 15, Stockmeyer gave Steiner a report on the results of his three-week trip. The preliminary group of teachers was put together and invited to participate in the training course. During the course it would become clear who the final teachers would be. In the end there were twelve. Stockmeyer was allowed to speak as their representative at the festive opening of the school on September 7. As he wrote in his autobiography, "The boundless enthusiasm of all participants has made the founding of the Waldorf school possible."

That which had seemed unachievable in the exchange between Charlemagne and his counselor was fulfilled at the founding of the Waldorf school. Emil Molt and Karl Stockmeyer were assisted in their 'human work' in all openness by the great initiate Rudolf Steiner. I hope that also our enthusiasm for this world-historic event can flame up again and again, for I am convinced that only this enthusiasm can be the flame for the future of the Waldorf school movement.

7

THE COURT SCHOOL OF CHARLEMAGNE

*A*lcuin was the man who gave the impetus for the founding of the Court School. Besides him there were many teachers working there. Many of these were given a second name in addition to their real name. Charlemagne himself was called David, and Alcuin had the name Flaccus, the name of the Roman poet Horace. Einhard had the name Bezaleel, Paulinus of Aquileia became Timothy, and Theodulf of Orleans became Pindar. Rotrud, Charles' favorite daughter, got the name Columba. Other scholars at the court included Peter of Pisa and Paul the Deacon.

The Court School was in Aachen where the cathedral (Dom) and the school formed an architectural unity. In this form we can detect the objective of the school. Odo of Metz was probably the architect who realized the structure in consultation with Charles and Alcuin. In the lower part of the Pfalz Chapel we find the following inscription: "This incomparable hall of honor was founded by the great emperor Charles and was executed by the learned master Odo who lies buried in Metz."

The construction of the Münster Church in Aachen (Fresco from 1858–1860, Josef Kehren after Alfred Rethel)

Odo of Metz executed Alcuin's vision of a temple for Christian arts and sciences. Beside the square stood a royal hall that would also have offered space for the Court School. A recent study by Hausmann[19] shows that the ground plan was based primarily on the circle, the square and the octagon. We will come back to these geometric principles when we contemplate how they connect with the curriculum.

In order to get to know the several teachers better, we will take a look at some of their poems. First we will hear Angilbert speak about the king and his beloved friends. He was a poet and a friend of Charles, and at court he had the name Homer.

> To Charlemagne and his companions
> Rise, pipe, and make sweet poems for my lord!
> David loves poetry; rise, pipe, and make poetry!
> David loves poets; David is the poets' glory,
> And so, all you poets join together in one,
> And sing sweet songs for my David!
> … Homer the poet loves David; make poetry, my pipe!
> … I greet you too, Gisela, God's holy virgin,
> Distinguished sister of David, in my never-ending poem
> … Hrothrud, a maiden celebrated for her intellect, loves poetry,
> She unites great beauty with high moral qualities.
> … Speak now with me, Muses, in praise of Bertha,
> May that excellent maiden like my poetry …
> [Hrothrud and Bertha are daughters of Charlemagne;
> Angilbert is in Bertha's service.]
> … Why should I not mention you, steward of the great court,
> For in you Aaron, once a great priest under Moses,
> Is now wondrously given a second life in our palace?
> You carry the ephod, the holy fire, to the altars,
> Bearing on your lips heaven's key, and in your hands the chapel key.
> With your prayers you constantly defend the people from the foe.
> [Aaron is the second name of Hildebald, later archbishop of
> Cologne.]
> …Thyrsis loves poetry, let us speak of Thyrsis in song,
> For his lofty faith shines from his white locks;
> Thyrsis' love glows from his pure heart,
> His sweet faith will make him dear to David.
> [Meginfrid, the valet, is called Thyrsis.]
> … Menalcas will come dripping from the rainy mountain

To read these verses and earn the court's affection;
Proper love of poets gleams in Menalcas' heart.
[Menalcas is Audulf, the seneschal.]
… First seeking the famous camps of Julius
And sing many kinds of poetic praise to that young man.
Then hurry back swiftly to this holy chapel,
Bearing on your lips the greetings of peace to all men.
[Julius is the name for Pepin, son of Charlemagne.]
… With Homer's love, greetings forever!
May omnipotent God preserve you forever and everywhere,
May Christ preserve you, David, forever!
David is our love, David is dear above all.
David loves poets, David is the poets' glory.
David loves Christ, Christ is David's glory.[20]

These quotations show how at Charlemagne's court names were used to express someone's being. Poetry and reality merge. This is especially striking in the indication and elaboration of Aaron as name for Hildebald, also called Hildebold. In her excellent study *Alcuin, Friend of Charlemagne*, Eleanor Shipley Duckett characterized many persons whose names are mentioned in these poems of Alcuin. [She also quotes all her sources. I chose to leave them out for the readability of the text – Trans.]

Hildebold, bishop of Cologne and arch-chaplain of the Court, blesses the board as priestly Aaron, the name by which he is known to all. From him, his "most familiar bishop," Charles at his dying was to receive the last Sacraments, "to fortify him for his going forth." Ercambald, chief secretary of the King, seizes two notebooks that hang by his side to take down dictation from Court officials.

Especially beloved by all was the seneschal [Audulf], or chief steward, who was made one of the fellowship of the Court by the name of Menalcas. He could be seen encompassed by squadrons of bakers and cooks, hurrying up the kitchen to send in Father Alcuin's special porridge, wiping sweat from his forehead, holding as it were a court of law over the menu. Beside him stood Thyrsis, the royal treasurer and chamberlain. His business it was, among

many duties, to admit and arrange the company; now he would
usher a guest promptly to his place with a smile and a bow,
now another would be bidden wait outside until room could
be prepared. Both Menalcas and Thyrsis, whose real name was
Megenfrid, respected deeply good verses and made a reverent
audience.

Angilbert wrote the following poem in 794. It formed the content of a letter
to Charles in which he compared the Court School with a garden:

> After reading this letter, run swiftly through the pleasant gardens,
> Where Homer used to live with his boys.
> See the beautiful flowers growing from the healthy grass,
> Whether they do well, whether they grow abundantly, whether
> The ravening foe does not break them with his cruel touch.
> See whether they are on all sides enclosed with strong hedges,
> Whether the house and the boys flourish, and the buildings too …

The picture of the garden used by Angilbert here in relation to the Court School
is something we can investigate further. Angilbert uses the picture with great
enthusiasm. The luxuriant, yet protected growth of plants and flowers transports
us to an atmosphere comparable to the 'Garden of Eden,' the 'earthly paradise.'
At the beginning of this chapter the architectural form of the Court School was
briefly mentioned. The paradisal garden can lead us to an understanding of the
architectural principle of the octagon
underlying the design of the Court Chapel.

In medieval architecture we always
find the octagon in relation to baptismal
chapels. It is the ideal form in which
to perform a baptism. The objective of
baptism is to enable the human being
to find his/her original condition again
through the sacramental act. This original
state was always represented by the image
of Adam and Eve in Paradise. It is the image
of the human being before the fall into sin

*A cross section of the
Münster Church in Aachen*

that lives in a form based on the octagon. Clemens of Alexandria expressed this in the 4th century as follows: "He whom Christ brings back to life is transformed into eightness."[21] In the Middle Ages Christ was experienced as the one who bestows the strength on the individual human being to restore the condition in which (s)he was before the fall. For that reason Paul called Christ 'the new Adam.'

The octagon of the Court Chapel was related to the Court School. It was the goal of the teaching in the Court School to awaken the human being in his original essence. In the names the teachers gave each other in this school we can recognize a similar gesture. In the second name they sought the higher being of the other. The everyday human being was placed in an ideal image which could also be an inspiration for the person himself in his task of learning.

As we have seen, Alcuin gave the impetus to these new names. In the following quotations from a poem by Alcuin on the Court School we can recognize his motives for several of these names.

> Your kind letter came from court,
> Most sweet David, beloved of God, bearing
> To me, Flaccus, the welcome news of your good health
> Which I hope almighty God will always increase.
> You are a source of praise, hope and joy to all your kingdom,
> You are an ornament to the church, its ruler, defender and lover.
> You have appointed deacons thoroughly worthy of their station
> In a sacred hierarchy to determined places in the chapel.
> See how the priests of Christ carry out their proper duties
> And his deacons perform their noble office,
> The sub deacons rejoicing in their dependable leaders.
> The doctors hurry up at once, disciples of Hippocrates,
> One taking blood from veins, one mixing herbs in a pot,
> One brewing poultices, and another serving potions.
> And yet, doctors, tend to everyone without charge,
> So that Christ may bless and guide your hands:
> Of all these things I approve, this is an order which I can praise.
> Was the poet Virgil the only one to do wrong at court?
> Did that distinguished man deserve not to have any teacher
> Who could assign fine poetry to the boys in the palace?
> What will Bezaleel, learned in the poems about Troy, do?

[As we have seen, Bezaleel is the second name of Einhard.
This was the name of the designer and builder of the Tabernacle
in which Moses kept the stone tablets with the Ten
          Commandments.]
Why, I ask, did he not direct the school in place of his father?
What about slow Drances with his white head of hair?
He is powerful in counsel, but his hand is too sluggish for warfare.
Little Zaccheus has climbed up in the tall tree
To watch the crowd of scribes running about,
With small letters and parchment he provides help to the needy.
May the boys look out and not lay hands on bribes!
[Alcuin is clearly concerned about Zaccheus, as also about Bezaleel
and Drances. Zaccheus is the second name of Ercambald,
the head of the Chancel.]
For every rank now has its own master:
An excellent, full-hearted priest
Governing others in deed and word,
Going before them and setting a distinguished example of salvation.
A succession of servants follows the master Jesse
Whose bull-like voice may resound in the temple of Christ,
As is proper for one who reads to the people God's word from on
          high.
After him Sulspicius the reader leads out his white-robed ranks;
May he guide and teach them not to err about fixed quantities.
[A reference to arithmetic?]
Idithun has taught the children holy chant,
So that they sing sweet sounds with sonorous voices.
Let them learn the feet, numbers and rhythms in which music
          consists!
May my daughter …
[Guntrada, daughter of Charlemagne, was Alcuin's pupil. Alcuin
wrote "De Anima Ratione" for her.]
… at night-time gaze upon the stars in the sky
And grow accustomed to giving constant praise to mighty God
Who arrayed the heavens with stars and the earth with grass,
And by His Word performed all the miracles in the world.
[Alcuin wrote letters to Charlemagne about the stars and planets.]

Flaccus' pipe will now compose a poem specially dedicated to you,
Homer, until you return to the sacred court.
May Thyrsis and Menalcas always be well,
And Menalcas chide the cooks in the black hall,
So that Flaccus has hot porridge in regular courses.
Let Nemias …
[Eppinus-Eberhard, the cup-bearer]
… fill his goblet with Greek wine,
For he is always accustomed to carry a barrel with him….[22]

The following quotations are all from E.S. Duckett, *Alcuin, Friend of Charlemagne* and give further illustrations of the various personalities at the court of Charlemagne.

> The wine was poured by Eppinus [Eberhard], who seems to have been called Nemias, or Nehemiah, restorer of the City.

> Einhard was living at court for instruction under wardship of the King. Alcuin who taught him, gave him the name Bezeleel, for he was filled with the Spirit of God to devise cunning works of gold, silver and brass in all manners of workmanship. Einhard was a maker of verses, also "skilled in Homeric strains." But everyone, and Alcuin included, called him in play Nardulus [Dwarfling] for his little stature. They always added, however, that he had a great mind. Alcuin compared him to the eye that rules the movements of the whole body; so, he jests, does Nardulus rule all the Palace.

> Among all, when Alcuin arrived in 782, none was more reverenced than the Queen Mother, Bertrada. She died the next year, in July 783, and was buried with great pomp and ceremony among the kings of Frankland at St. Denis. Shortly before, on the eve of Ascension Day in the same year, Charles had lost his Queen Hildegard. …She was only twelve years old when he married her and in the twelve years of their wedded life she bore him nine children. …Of her children Alcuin saw six grow up. …Rotrud [Hrothrud]—'Columba, the Dove of Peace'—grew up as a quiet and serious girl, not striking or handsome in appearance. For

many years she lived under her aunt Gisela, abbess of the double monastery of Chelles. Alcuin wrote letters. …There they gained from this "dear teacher and father" his commentary on the Gospel of Saint John.

Son Pepin we have seen baptized in Rome by Pope Hadrian at Eastertide 781, anointed and crowned King of Italy. He remained most of his boyhood in Italy. …Perhaps it was for this that Alcuin called him Julius.

A special partiality seems to have linked Alcuin with the third boy, twin of the dead Chlotar (who died as a young child), who did succeed his father's empire as Louis 'the Pious.' He was shy and retiring, unlike his high-spirited brothers, and loved to consult Alcuin on matters of religion and conscience. Soon after birth, he too had been crowned with Pepin by Hadrian at Rome, as King of Aquitaine.

The third daughter, Gisela, he renamed Delia. Alcuin records that Delia was skilled in music, and he writes to her in jest that he finds comfort for her neglect of him in the poetry of Virgil.

Berta: she was the most attractive of the three. …By her charm she won the heart of Angilbert, the constant companion and counselor of Charles. …To Alcuin, like her sisters, this Berta was his "dearest daughter," but unlike them, she comes to us with no name of his bestowing.

Chief, however, of Alcuin's friends among women in Frankland was the elder Gisela, sister of Charles, the abbess of Chelles. Alcuin wrote to her as Lucia. …She was a keen student of sacred books.

These three, Peter [of Pisa], Paul [the Deacon], and Paulinus [of Aquileia, see chapter 11] were leaders of discussions in humanities for Charles and his kinsfolk at the Palace in 782, the date of Alcuin's arrival… Angilbert listened to the discourses of Peter, of Paul and of Alcuin: He placed before their critical eyes his early efforts in verse. …The Kind, like all the Court, called him Homer, a name doubtless bestowed by Alcuin, and held him, as a royal letter to the Pope put it, to be "the counselor of my intimate and private ear."

Adalhard, abbot of the monastery of Saint Peter and Paul, Corbie, was of the royal family, a cousin of the King. Alcuin knew him well and called him Antony, for he was taught as a child and youth in the Palace School. His brother, Wala [see chapter 25 on Rudolf Hauschka], too, and his sister, Guntrada, were present at its discussions; and Alcuin acknowledged their part in its fellowship by renaming them Arsenius and Eulalia.

As we can see, the second naming of everyone given by Alcuin was to build a fellowship, which had a strong social structure and can be characterized in a spirit of freedom and open mind.

8

Goosefoot Berta and Daniel van Bemmelen

Daniel or Daan van Bemmelen was one of the first pioneers of Waldorf education in Holland and a cofounder of the first Waldorf school in The Hague. Toward the end of his life he had to undergo two operations. When he woke up after one of these, he experienced a female figure from the time of Charlemagne and later was able to tell who this woman was. He was convinced that he had experienced the mother of Charlemagne, Bertrada or Berta—'Goosefoot' Berta.[23]

Who was this mother of Charlemagne? If we look for the trail to her father we will also find the way to her spiritual signature. For Bertrada was the daughter of the great Christian initiate Charibert de Laon. We know this historical personality under the name of Flor from the medieval story of Flor and Blanchefleur. Rudolf Steiner indicated that this historical personality concealed the individuality of St. John the Evangelist. In a later incarnation Charibert reappeared as the founder of the Rosicrucians, Christian Rosenkreutz.[24]

Daan van Bemmelen

What was the impulse Berta adopted from her father? Surprisingly it is possible to answer this question quite directly. Her impulse was the fairy tales of Mother Goose of which tradition says they go back to Charlemagne's mother,

Berta who was known for her big, possibly six-toed 'goose feet.' These fairy tales of Mother Goose were edited and published under this name by the Frenchman Charles Perrault. They include Red Riding Hood, Snow-White, Cinderella, Hansel and Gretel and many others. Again, it was Steiner who pointed out that the origin of the fairy tales lies in the temples of the Rosicrucians.[25] That means that Berta must have heard them from her father. And as we know as lower school teachers, the fairy tales contain great, wisdom-filled initiation motifs. Daan van Bemmelen made an exhaustive study of Berta, which makes it possible to form a more concrete picture of her life before she married Pepin, Charlemagne's father.

In three extant versions dating from the 13th century, Berta is described as the daughter of Flor and Blanchefleur, king and queen of Hungary. Although she is destined to marry Pepin the Short, through fraud the latter first marries another woman while Berta is condemned to death. Fortunately the sentence is not executed, and she is able to hide with friendly people. After a lot of intrigue the truth comes to light and the false bride and her helper are convicted. Berta then marries Pepin and becomes Charlemagne's mother after first bearing a daughter who becomes the mother of Roland, the valiant friend of Charlemagne who fell at Ronceval.

Thus we see two lines of descent. The legend goes back to the royal house of Hungary, to the legendary but in an esoteric sense very important Flor and Blanchefleur. Side by side with this, it is historically certain that Berta was the daughter of Charibert de Laon and was born in Samoussy near Laon in France. But both stories are not necessarily mutually exclusive. In later incarnations, Christian Rosenkreutz was known often to change his name, title and home, for instance in his incarnation as the Count of St. Germain in the 18th century.

Charibert is known to have founded many monasteries and schools that were open to the groups of Irish and Anglo-Saxon monks who still traveled around Europe. In these monastic schools the art of handwriting books (calligraphy) was taught. They also made many Greek writings, such as, for instance, the doctrine of the nine hierarchies by Dionysius the Areopagite, accessible to medieval spiritual life for the first time. These monasteries formed a lively source of spiritual life in which the Irish-Celtic spirit brought a new impulse. In the first chapter it was mentioned that in the 7th century the Celtic folk spirit took on a new task by becoming the spirit of Grail Christianity. This being of the Grail was nurtured in the monasteries founded by Charibert. In a harmonious relationship between art and spiritual science Charibert and his followers served the Grail.

The cathedral school in Laon formed the center of twelve such initiatives all located in eastern France and Luxemburg. The impulse originated in Prüm on the border between Luxemburg and Germany.[26] In the local tourist office there hangs a large 19th century painting showing Charibert as a boy together with his mother, who also had the name Berta (Bertrada), signing the proclamation of the founding of the monastery of Prüm.

Bertrada

Bertrada and Charibert sign the
founding proclamation.
(Detail of painting in tourist office,
Prüm, Luxemburg)

Goosefoot Berta carried the impulse of her father further. In the arts of fairytale telling and of practical spinning that she guarded at the court of her spouse, and later of her son Charlemagne, the essence of esoteric Christianity lived which was found in the image of the Grail. Berta clothed the Grail teaching in fairytale pictures. For Charlemagne the counsel of his mother was very important. He held her in high honor and she had great influence at court. She must most certainly have kept watch over the Rome-oriented teachers so they would not have too much influence. This made it possible that at the height of the Carolingian court school there could be a certain harmonious collaboration between the representatives of the more exoterically oriented teachers, including

Einhard, Charlemagne's biographer and one of his leading advisors,[27] and those of Grail Christianity who often continued to work out of the Irish-Celtic impulse. Waldo von Reichenau was the great representative of this second stream, which harkened back to Charibert/Flor.

For Daan van Bemmelen, the inner connection with Berta in the last years of his life was a source of enthusiasm and strength. Around the time of the founding of the Waldorf teachers training college on Choisy Street in Zeist, Daan was living intensively with the spiritual image of Berta. The conviction grew in him that he was connected in a karmic sense with this important female figure around Charlemagne. The founding of this college was the crown on the work that began with the Waldorf school in The Hague. It was not without significance for Daan that the teachers college was located on Choisy Street, for Choisy (a town in France) was the place where Goosefoot Berta died. In Carolingian times it had been Berta's endeavor to connect the spiritual impulse of Grail Christianity with the budding and growing individual intelligence of European humanity. Out of the wealth of images of the fairy tales, she was the guardian of the spiritual content of the Carolingian school impulse. Collaborating with those who worked out of the more intellectual, Rome-oriented principle was not always easy for her.

In somewhat different words the same thing can be said of the work of Daan van Bemmelen within the framework of the Waldorf school movement. Daan too lived in great, wide-ranging pictures. In part because of his friendship with Walter Johannes Stein, the theme of the Grail was very close to his heart. As an artist (painter), Daan had found his way to Waldorf pedagogy and anthroposophy at a young age when he heard both Steiner and Emil Molt speak in Holland. Especially the words and the being of Emil Molt gave him a decisive impetus toward his future profession. After Emil Molt's lecture he knew for sure: "I am going to be a Waldorf teacher!" And just as Goosefoot Berta was not only the daughter of a great Christian initiate but also his trusted pupil, Daan found in Rudolf Steiner his spiritual teacher.

One more motif in Daan's life must be mentioned. When Daan was in art school as a young man in Amsterdam, he went through a serious crisis. At that time of deep inner darkness, the Gospel of St. John became a support for him and it helped him come out of this deep, dark place. Now, as we saw, it was Berta's father in whom the author of this gospel came back to life.[28] Rudolf Steiner, and with him Christian Rosenkreutz, were very close to Daan's heart and, through him, also to the heart of the Dutch Waldorf school movement. We may hope that people like Daan van Bemmelen can remain connected with the movement in a spiritual sense to help our pedagogy retain a character that is carried by the spiritual world.

9

The Destiny of the
Waldorf School Movement

The following is an address given by Daan van Bemmelen at the festive opening of the Free Pedagogical Academy (the Waldorf teachers training college in Holland) on September 3, 1974. Daan van Bemmelen was one of the founders of the first Waldorf school in The Hague, Holland, in 1923.

When people on earth want to start an organization they do that out of ideas they received during their life before birth and which they developed together with higher spiritual angel beings. The ideas are the result of resolutions of will which they carried through the portal of death after their previous lives on earth. The time and place of the realization of these pre-birth impulses depend on those spiritual beings who determine destiny (karma). And the individual karma of the human being, in turn, depends on the world karma of all of humanity.

The Lord of world karma is Christ, who connected Himself with all of humanity after the Mystery of Golgotha. But there are not only good spiritual beings, those who serve the Lord of world karma; there are also evil ones who oppose Him. St. John shows this to us in the mighty pictures of the Book of Revelation—the enormous battle behind the scenes of world history between the hosts of the Good and those of Evil. The hosts of the Good are led by the prince of the archangels, Michael, and those of Evil by Ahriman/Satan, also called the Great Dragon. That which St. John described in the 10th chapter of Revelations is now beginning to become reality, because in 1879 Michael assumed his high position of leading time spirit.

The people who found organizations on earth are not always conscious of their intentions, and even less so of the karmic conditions of their impulses. But in the first quarter of the last century Steiner was working, who may be called the great teacher of karma and reincarnation. I would like to give a personal example here of the way I came to consciousness through him.

When my wife and I wanted to start the Waldorf school in The Hague, we asked Rudolf Steiner for his approval; his answer was: "If it is your will." I did not understand him because I thought it was self-evident that it was our will. We asked if he would give his approval. When he replied with the same words, I asked him with some emphasis whether he thought we were the right people for this school. He then answered roughly as follows: "It is not just a question of will, but also of being resolved to follow through and bring to completion what you have decided to do." How often is our will not just a longing, an illusion or a momentary flush? When difficulties and disappointments then come, we just give up, walk away and start something else.

I am glad Steiner taught us to persist despite all adversity and bitter experience, for at this time the Waldorf schools are a recognized movement of educational renewal that is continually expanding.

The karma of the Dutch Waldorf schools[29] is part of the world karma underlying the first Waldorf school in Stuttgart. When we want to find the origin of this karma we must go back to the 8th and 9th centuries, the time of Charlemagne who lived from 742 to 814. In history books we can read that Charlemagne founded the first schools in his realm, and that he learned to read and write himself, something highly unusual for a king in his day.

He received the impulse for founding schools from his mother Berta, or Bertrada, 'with the big feet,' also called Mother Goose. Many well-known fairy tales were first told by her. Her father had the name Charibert de Laon and he may be called the spiritual leader of the 8th century. He was a count in the realm of the Franks, but he also descended from the Gauls, the ancient Celtic inhabitants of France who fought the Romans for many, many years.

Many of the deep insights into the world of the stars, of nature and the seasons possessed by the Druids, the Celtic priests, were also living in the soul of Charibert de Laon. But he had connected these insights with the message the Irish-Scottish preachers had brought about the Sun God, who had made his abode in a son of humanity and had thus overcome death.

This cosmic Christianity was taught in the Hibernian (Irish) mystery temples, and Columbanus with his twelve followers first brought it from the island of Iona to France, Alsace, Switzerland and Italy. These monks preached in the vernacular, not in Latin, and their teaching was independent of church dogma from Rome. The Hibernian mysteries still taught knowledge of divine hierarchies which we can also find in the letters of St. Paul. A written copy of this doctrine of nine heavenly hierarchies, which goes back to Dionysius the Areopagite, had been given by the Byzantine emperor to Charlemagne and was kept in the monastery of St. Denis near Paris.

They also knew the Greek philosophy of the Logos, the creative Word of God, which we find in the prologue of the Gospel of St. John. These works were read in Greek. In addition, the Hibernian mystery centers taught the wisdom of the ancient mysteries and of the Gnosis that was the world view of the first theologians in the 1st century AD. All of this lived in the souls of the Celtic preachers who travelled in Europe.

All Gnostic schools and ancient mysteries were eradicated by Rome in the 4th century, and their teaching was declared heretical. Nevertheless it spread east and west in heretical sects. But also a mystery temple arose, partly on earth, partly in the spiritual world, where human initiates together with angel beings guarded the true gnosis which encompassed the greatest mystery, the mystery of Golgotha, until humanity would be mature enough to receive it. In the 8th century world karma had matured to the point that this knowledge could be revealed to humanity, not in intellectual form but through the feeling life, in sagas and legends. Charibert de Laon was one of those who were able to receive this revelation.

The first legend he spread was the one of Flor and Blanchefleur. This legend relates how the Moorish prince Flor went to the Arabic world to search for his lost bride where she was held captive in the harem of a sultan. When he was smuggled into her room in a basket full of red roses, he was found out and sentenced to immediate beheading. As the executioner raised his sword to lop off his head, he was interrupted because Blanchefleur put her own head on the block. There now developed such a noble contest between the two lovers for who would be the first to be beheaded that all the spectators were moved and the sultan granted both of them their lives.

Behind this legend is concealed the fact that Charibert sent an embassy to Arabia in order to bring the gnostic wisdom, which was still being taught in Arab schools, to Europe. The symbol of the red rose, Flor,[30] indicates the sun power of Christ who dwells in the heart's blood of the human being. The symbol of the white lily, Blanchefleur (literally white flower) conceals the moon wisdom of the Orient as head capacity. The lily opens solely for the sun warmth of Christian love.

Another legend Charibert de Laon spread, the legend of the Grail, brings to expression how angels brought the gnostic secret of the Mystery of Golgotha from a hidden place in the Orient to the West. The sacred jasper vessel Christ used when he broke bread at the last supper, and in which Joseph of Arimathea collected the blood of Jesus that symbolized the Mystery of Golgotha, was preserved by angels until Titurel built the Grail Temple and they could bring the Holy Grail down to humanity. Later, in the 12th century, this legend was written down by Robert de Boron.

These legends of Flor and Blanchefleur and of the Grail lived in the hearts of Charlemagne's grandfather and his mother. At his court Grail Christianity was represented by Irish-Scottish monks, especially by Waldo von Reichenau. They stood in contrast to Einhard who advocated Roman Christianity. Influenced by Waldo, Charlemagne embarked on a serious study of Germanic-Frankish languages, wrote a Frankish grammar, and gave the months of the year and the winds Frankish names. He also sponsored a collection of Germanic songs and hero sagas. In the schools Latin was taught in deference to the servants of the church. The organization of the schools was entrusted to Alcuin from Britain who introduced the Greek method of the Seven Liberal Arts of Gnostic science.

In this way Charlemagne made great efforts to unite the two streams, the Celtic esoteric one and the Roman exoteric one. But those who represented the latter did what they could to tie him more and more to Rome. It was against his will that to his surprise he was crowned emperor by Pope Leo III at Christmas 800 in Rome. But only after Charlemagne's death did the followers of the Roman stream succeed in eliminating all representatives of Grail Christianity. Even their names were crossed out in the official books.

Grail Christianity now withdrew into secrecy again. Those who stood in this stream carried their impulses either through death or through spiritual schooling into the Grail Temple which was invisible and not to be found by the outer world. There they awaited as Grail Knights the arrival of a new initiate who would be capable of redeeming humanity from its suffering that was caused by its refusal to accept the Mystery of Golgotha. This is the story of Parsifal who healed king Amfortas from his illness and was proclaimed king. The saga did not become public until the 12th century, but it took place in actual reality in the 9th century, as is clearly indicated by Wolfram von Eschenbach in his epic poem. He relates that Herzeleide, Parsifal's mother, lived eleven generations before him.

The souls that belonged to both streams under Charlemagne were born again in the centuries after 1200. They worked both within the Church and in heretical sects, and opposed each other. After that time all these souls gathered around the archangel Michael in a spiritual mystery school, where Michael showed them in mighty images how they were to bring Grail Christianity into earthly reality in the 20th century.

When Steiner was teaching anthroposophy, when his mystery dramas were performed and the Goetheanum was being built, many people experienced an awakening of memories of prior lives, and also of resolutions of will they had carried through the portal of death and of experiences in the supersensible Michael school.

Emil Molt was one of those who were thus seized by the impulse when he asked Steiner to set up a school for the children of the workers in his Waldorf Astoria cigarette factory. In 1919 Steiner gave three two-week courses to the first group of teachers he had selected, and he opened the school with a solemn ceremony, in which he invoked the blessing of the good spiritual beings who serve the living Christ, and who want to help human beings to seek Him, receive Him and carry Him further from eternity to eternity.

10

HERBERT HAHN WORKING IN THE SPIRIT OF WALDO VON REICHENAU

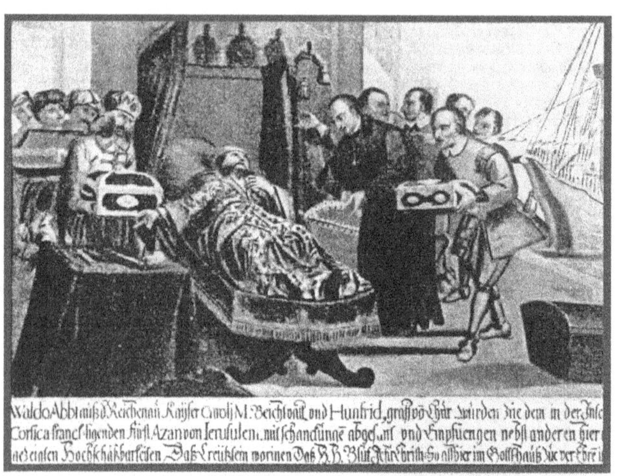

*Waldo von Reichenau receiving the Blood of Christ from the
dying guardian of the relic.
(Painting in the church of Reichenau-Mittelzell)*

*H*erbert Hahn relates how he worked in the factory of Emil Molt giving courses to the workers during their work hours. Here he got to know Emil Molt, and when the impulse for the Waldorf school arose out of the impulse toward social threefolding, Herbert Hahn was one of the first collaborators. He was born in Pertau, Estonia, on May 5, 1890. His biographer, Johannes Tautz, calls this town one of many languages where Estonians, Germans and Russians met.

Later, Herbert would master many languages. The connection this gave him with all peoples of Europe would at the end of his life lead him to write his book *Vom Genius Europas*. After finishing high school and starting his studies at the University of Estonia, he left for Germany to study linguistics and philosophy in Heidelberg. Here he heard his first lecture by Rudolf Steiner on January 21, 1909:

Someone said to me: "Trying to reform life is well and good, but it is no more than an outer appearance that requires an inner process. I know someone who has a lot to say about this inner process. He is soon coming to Heidelberg to give a lecture, and you should by all means attend it." In this way I heard that a man called Rudolf Steiner would soon speak in the city auditorium about Goethe's secret revelation.

At that time Herbert Hahn had two life questions. The first was: What is the true nature of the human being? And the second was the question of what challenges our time was posing for humanity.[31] In the lecture both of these questions were addressed, and from that moment his connection with the person and work of Steiner started to grow.

In 1911 he continued his studies in Berlin, and "now finally I read a little publication by Rudolf Steiner I had carried around for years. Its title was *The Lord's Prayer, An Esoteric Study.*" He read it with great intensity and recognized the truth it expressed. Later he would stand at the root of religious instruction in the Waldorf schools and, together with Steiner, would shape the Sunday services for children. Now the seed was planted. The booklet on the Lord's Prayer brought him the image of the human being that would later be the basis of his work as a Waldorf school teacher.

In the same period, during a trip through Italy, he also met the Russian poet Maxim Gorki. From him he heard the saying: "We have to learn to learn." When he was eighty years old he would speak these words again relative to the students and teachers of the Waldorf school who were assembled to celebrate his birthday.

In 1912 followed several personal conversations with Steiner. He was asked to investigate the essence of the word and the various languages in relation to the various folk souls. Another subject that came up in these conversations was the *Calendar of the Soul* that had just then appeared. In virtually all Waldorf schools in the world, the teachers begin the day by reading one of these weekly verses. In this conversation about the *Calendar of the Soul,* Herbert Hahn received an insight that would prove decisive for his life. Through Steiner he came to the realization that he could orient himself on the power of the I. From that moment he was convinced of the creative power that emanates from the human I and also reveals itself in language.

After his graduation Hahn went to Russia to teach French, then switched to German and finally decided to return to Germany to study for his doctorate. When he reached the border he heard of the assassination in Sarajevo which shortly led to the eruption of World War I. When in Kassel he had another conversation with Steiner whom he met again a few years later in 1919 on the grounds of the cigarette factory of Emil Molt. "There you are finally!" were the words with which Steiner received him. Such was the path that led him to his life's goal his twenty-ninth year. In that year the founding of the first Waldorf school became a reality, in part because of his efforts.

Who was Herbert Hahn, and what was the creative force that emanated from him? Steiner indicated the creative force of the I to him. He also lived intensively with the Lord's Prayer. And this force again and again awakened in him his interest in the power of the word, the way it reveals itself in the various peoples in Europe.

At the court school of Charlemagne the teachers who were Irish-Celtic oriented encouraged Alcuin to stimulate the teaching in the respective local languages side by side with Latin, which was then the international language. Charles told Alcuin to collect and write down the sagas and stories about the gods of the Saxon peoples. Without this influence many stories, which we now know under the name of the *Edda*, and which are told in the fourth grade of the Waldorf schools, would surely have been completely lost.

Still, it was not easy for the Irish-Celtic oriented teachers to persist in this impulse because another stream, more directed by Rome, considered this kind of teaching destructive. This stream wished to place everything under the authority of the pope. This led to a conflict within the College of Teachers of the court school. Beside Alcuin, Waldo von Reichenau was working as a representative of the faction that favored teaching in the languages of the people. Charlemagne valued him highly. And yet he is practically forgotten in history. Fortunately, in 1857 a certain Phillip Herber pulled this great teacher out of oblivion. In his study of Waldo von Reichenau, he writes:[32]

Waldo, abbot of St. Gallen and protestant, became abbot of Reichenau, bishop of Pavia [Italy] and finally abbot of St. Denis [Paris]. He died in 814. We first heard of Waldo that he was elected abbot of St. Gallen in a free election in 780, and was acknowledged in this position by Charlemagne. He was praised in the annals of the monastery as an exemplary writer.

At that time a certain Egino was bishop of Constance who professed to have a claim on St. Gallen. He had great power and became so coercive relative to the abbot that the latter took the matter to the king, defending his position on the basis of the founding charter of the monastery. Also daily practice confirmed the independence of the monastery of St. Gallen. But according to the annals of St. Gallen, Egino, who had obtained a copy of the charter under false pretenses, had falsified it.

The king then tried to bring about a unification of the Germanic [sic] and Roman church orientations, hoping in this way to reconcile the two parties. As abbot of St. Gallen, Waldo would then be the highest authority, but in accordance with the capitulars Egino would have overarching control. Waldo objected to that. He foresaw the future of the monastery if it lost its ecclesiastical freedom. With great conviction he declared: "As long as I can use these three fingers, I will never subject myself to the bishop." As explained by the reporter, he indicated the three fingers with which he wrote. He would rather live from writing books than place the free monastery and himself, as abbot working under the rules of Columba, under the authority of the bishop of Constance. He would rather give up his position and, in the end, he resigned as abbot, and thus as leader of the monastery school.

Thus ended Waldo's work in St. Gallen. Under him the school had grown large and famous. Fortunately the Irish spirit did not disappear, but was continued by Notker and Liutward (see chapter 12). But the story of his life continues:

We see him again in Reichenau, the beautiful monastery on the Rhine; in 786 he is elected abbot there and acknowledged by Charlemagne. According to the famous chronicle of 'Lahmen Hermann,' he fulfilled this function for twenty years, until 806.

Schönhuth describes the time when Waldo was abbot as follows in his chronicle of the monastery of Reichenau:[33]

The time of Waldo was the true beginning of the practice of the sciences in Reichenau. Since that time the landscape there was

rich not only in earthly but also in spiritual goods. He founded
schools following the example of St. Gallen, where the school was
for young men who wanted to devote themselves to the sciences
without any other special purpose [such as becoming a priest –
FL]. Very soon the number of students was so large that the school
could accept only counts and other noblemen.

Under Waldo's leadership 640 monks lived in the monastery. This
probably included the counts and noblemen who left again after
a certain time. Waldo gave the schools excellent teachers and did
everything he could to stimulate the arts and sciences. He was
able to do this because he possessed a large quantity of books. He
brought a number of these to the monastery himself, and when
he was charged with the bishopric of Pavia in Italy, he acquired
a number of books. Special mention must be made here of the
Antiphonarium he received as a gift from Bertrada, the mother
of Charlemagne. He also commissioned books for his own use.
His scientific striving was not limited to the theological sciences,
but extended also to the other sciences that were practiced in the
monastery, the so-called Humaniores.

After Waldo had been in function for twenty years, Charlemagne
entrusted him with the leadership of the monastery of St. Denis in
Paris.

In this monastery Charlemagne and Waldo composed a document with the
purpose of guaranteeing religious freedom. The old emperor finally spoke himself
of a reformation of the church.[34] In the end, in 813, the order went out that in
the churches in his realm, the sermon was to be spoken in German. Charlemagne
liked to visit Waldo in St. Denis. This is apparent from the fact that on a visit to
Waldo in 811 the Irishman Dungal explained to Charles why there had been two
sun eclipses in 810. About Waldo the following was said:

Waldo belonged to the most radiant stars. First was he a monk,
then an abbot. He spread the light of his insights into far distant
lands. Although he was born into the highest nobility, as a monk
he diligently studied theology. On the ground of his exceptional

insights Charlemagne made him abbot and his personal confessor and advisor in 786. In addition to Ludger, Waldo was a Court Chaplain. He survived Ludger by four years and died two months after the death of his friend Charlemagne.[35]

All his life, Herbert Hahn felt himself connected with the life of Waldo. His friend and colleague at the Waldorf school, Walter Johannes Stein, described in his book, *The Ninth Century*, a Grail legend around the life and striving of Waldo von Reichenau. He recognized the same impulse Waldo displayed toward searching and striving in its continuation in his friend Herbert Hahn during the forming and building of the Waldorf school. Stein was also the one who found Phillip Heber's book on Waldo.

Waldo stood in the center of the conflict between the Roman and Irish influences on the school impulse of Charlemagne. Today Waldorf school teachers can also fully experience this conflict in the way we handle freedom of education and the demands of the state. Until his death on June 20, 1970, Herbert Hahn worked with all his forces to build a Waldorf school movement that was spiritually able to operate in the several countries of Europe and elsewhere within the local customs and languages. His work carried the signature of the Grail impulse. This came to expression in the way he, together with Steiner, gave form to the "Sunday Service for Children" as a service without connection to any established church.

In conclusion I want to quote a part of the letter Herbert Hahn wrote to Daan van Bemmelen in Holland when the Waldorf school in The Hague had just been started in 1923. The college of teachers in Stuttgart had been following the founding of this school with great attention and warmth. On September 13 Herbert Hahn wrote the following on behalf of the college of teachers:

> Dear good Friends!
> We feel connected with you in much love and friendship. I
> remember fondly the beautiful hours I spent in Haarlem and The
> Hague. Inwardly I am building a bridge to you not only from soul
> to soul, but also to the landscape with which I feel connected.
> Across mountains and moors to the sea! Yesterday we felt intimately
> connected with you. Blessings on your work! Our college thinks
> of you!

Herbert Hahn

On November 2, 1923, Herbert Hahn wrote another extensive letter to Daan. It is an example of the strong bond of confidence existing between the teachers of the two schools. Hahn gave a report of a conversation he had had with Walter Johannes Stein, an intimate conversation in the sign of the Grail and the renewed working of the Grail community in our time. This community works out of the time spirit Michael in service of the future of the earth.

Walter Johannes Stein found his way to us. I came into conversation with him in remarkable circumstances. We spoke together for three hours. Step by step he showed the depth of his soul. In it the impulse revealed itself to which we have to give the answer. A change took place in his inner life after he had been lonely for months and had experienced that consciously. He has often meditated about the significance of the heart in relation to the Grail. He then came to inner experiences that said to him: "You must learn to turn from book knowledge to the human being himself. You must learn to keep silent on that which lives in your soul."

In a dream he was told: "Go the way from Gabriel to Michael!" With immense effort he found and went this way. He showed me a note in his diary: "I have decided to meditate on Michael."

This conversation was a magnificent experience for me. It is the crown on the conversations we have had over the years.

Waldo von Reichenau and his friend Hunfrid present Charlemagne with the Blood of Christ. (Painting in the church of Reichenau-Mittelzell)

11

WIDUKIND AND CHARLEMAGNE – "WHERE IS WIDUKIND"?

*T*he connection of the Waldorf school movement with the educational impulse of Charlemagne may lead to the question of where Widukind might be, the leader of the Saxons against which Charlemagne had to wage a protracted war. This question is interesting because it will move our attention from the destiny of the teachers to that of the pupils of the first Waldorf school.

My point of departure is an incident that occurred in the tenth grade to Walter Johannes Stein, the first history teacher. It is related in a letter of February 4, 1952, from Stein to Emil Bock, the leader of The Christian Community at the time. Stein describes the following:

> I was telling the children how Widukind, the duke of the
> Saxons, came into the church in Aachen and how, when he saw
> the monstrance, he called out: "Saxnot."[36] Upon hearing that,
> Charlemagne embraced him and reconciled himself with him. It
> made a deep impression on the children. Dr. Steiner said to me
> about this: "No wonder; they were the Saxons who were there."[37]

In the same letter Stein tells Bock that Steiner added: "The teachers are Aristotelians and the pupils are Saxons from the time of Charlemagne."

Widukind was the leader of the Saxons who time and again rebelled against Charlemagne. Between 772 and 804 repeated wars took place between Saxons and Franks. A dramatic climax in these wars took place with the beheading of 4500 rebellious Saxons in Verden, an event Charlemagne would regret for the rest of his life. Ever after the first invasion by Charlemagne in 772, Widukind always knew to foment another rebellion among the Saxons, and when Charlemagne tried to capture him, he always escaped to the territory of the friendly Danish king.

To get an insight in the character of Widukind and the Saxons, I am quoting here the description given by Einhard, the biographer and contemporary of Charlemagne:

> No war ever undertaken by the Frank nation was carried on with such persistence and bitterness, or cost so much labor, because the Saxons, like almost all the tribes of Germany, were a fierce people, given to the worship of devils, and hostile to our religion … Accordingly war was begun against them, and was waged for thirty-three successive years with great fury, more, however, to the disadvantage of the Saxons than of the Franks …
>
> It is hard to say how often they were conquered and, humbly submitting to the King, promised to do what was enjoined upon them, gave without hesitation the required hostages, and received the officers sent them from the King. They were sometimes so much weakened and reduced that they promised to renounce the worship of devils and to adopt Christianity, but they were no less ready to violate these terms than prompt to accept them …
>
> The war that had lasted so many years was at length ended by their acceding to the terms offered by the King, which were renunciation of their national religious customs and the worship of devils, acceptance of the sacraments of the Christian faith and religion, and union with the Franks to form one people.*

From this description it becomes clear how difficult the situation vis-à-vis the Saxons under Widukind must have been. It is noteworthy that Einhard does not mention the name of Widukind. Einhard wrote this biography later in his life when Widukind had ceased his resistance and was living in the last part of his life as a monk in the Irish-oriented monastery on the island of Reichenau in Lake Constance (between Germany and Switzerland).

In his monograph on Charlemagne, the German historian Rudolph Wahl gives a striking description that is, however, also a bit tendentious:

---

* Note: Einhard, *The Life of Charlemagne*, Part 7, Fordham.edu/hallsall/basis/einhard. html.

Widukind…, his name probably means Son of Wotan. He was
regarded as the principal nobleman in all of Saxony; he had
possessions everywhere and was immeasurably rich. His family
castle stood on the eastern border of Westphalia in Wildeshausen
on the confluence of the rivers Hunte and Weser. Because he was
the son-in-law of the Danish king Siegfried, his estates reached far
over the borders of Saxony. This ambitious man surpassed his fellow
tribesmen in intelligence to such an extent that he became more
and more suspicious in their eyes.

From a spiritual point of view, we could interpret Rudolph Wahl's insinuation
in a different way. Widukind's name indicates that he was an initiate in the
Germanic mysteries. Wotan is another name for Odin, the All-Father of the *Edda*.
Waldorf school children hear many stories about him in fourth grade. The name
of his father-in-law, Siegfried, also points in this direction. We know Siegfried
from the "Song of the Nibelungs" that appears in the curriculum of the tenth
grade and gives the students a second opportunity to meet the Norse gods which
they will recall from fourth grade.

Now, the story of the conversion of Widukind was told by Walter Johannes
Stein in the first tenth grade of the Waldorf school in Stuttgart. We know
about this class from the eyewitness account of Rudolf Grosse. His book *Erlebte
Pädagogik (Pedagogy Experienced)* appeared in 1968 and describes, among other
things, the lessons by Stein.

We know Rudolf Grosse in the Waldorf movement as the predecessor
of Jørgen Smit, Heinz Zimmermann and Christof Wiechert as leaders of the
pedagogical section at the Goetheanum in Dornach. Later he became head of the
General Anthroposophical Society. He died in the early 1980s. On May 1, 1922,
he joined the first tenth grade in Stuttgart, a decision he made completely on his
own. He left the gymnasium he had attended in Zurich on his own initiative.
His encounter with the Goetheanum in Dornach in April one year earlier is
characteristic:

It was April 1921, and some of us Wandervögel (wanderbirds) were
preparing an Easter trip. There were five of us, and our itinerary
led us through the Jura Mountains. None of us knew the area well,
but because our geography teacher had just recently described it

so well, we had become curious and wanted to get to know the region. The trip developed like so many others. We had engaging conversations about the school and the teachers, about important and less important subjects, we sang songs, we cooked our food and built our camps. We climbed the Jura Ridge, descended into deep clefts and came back up into delightful meadows, until in the end we reached the most northerly slopes of the Jura.

A magnificent spring day saw us walking on narrow field tracks among white-blossoming cherry trees when we suddenly through an opening in the trees saw a mighty building with two slate-covered domes that gleamed in the sun like none of us had seen before. My friend Viktor and I spontaneously said: "That's where we are going. We've got to see that." We were speechless when the others, equally determined, said: "Then you can go by yourselves. We have no interest in that elephant-temple!" None of us knew what Dornach was or what the Goetheanum meant, and none of us had ever heard of anthroposophy. Still, here a clear separation of spirits was taking place. It is a riddle I have thought about a lot ever since.

A little over a year later Rudolf Grosse mades his own decision, told his mother and became a pupil in the tenth grade in Stuttgart. It was a strange class. He describes:

The situation I found in the Waldorf school was remarkable. The tenth grade, to which I belonged since May 1, 1922, was the highest grade. It was taken further year by year and was therefore also the class for which Rudolf Steiner every year developed a new curriculum. This means that the teachers were also entering new and unknown territory every year. The same went for the pupils because they were also going through an unknown process. Before they had come to the Waldorf school, they had all gone to state schools, most of them outside Stuttgart in other parts of Germany and even abroad. This gave the class a colorful character in every respect. It had not yet become a whole.

In addition, there was the completely different way in which teachers and pupils interacted with each other than in the state schools. A kind of unrest reigned in the upper school, which clearly showed that the pupils had not yet found solid ground under their feet and also did not know how they should be behaving. Out of the strict, well-delineated forms of the other schools, they were now thrown together in a school where everything was in a state of becoming and still had to find its own form. And for the teachers it was no different.

But Rudolf Grosse felt at home. He was lucky, also as regards his lodging. He was taken into the family of Emil Molt. A close friendship developed with the son of the latter, Walter, who was in ninth grade. At mealtimes he always had

Rudolf Grosse

Walter J. Stein

Herbert Hahn

The first 12th Class in Stuttgart with Rudolf Grosse, Walter Johannes Stein and Herbert Hahn. Other teachers not in the photograph include Ernst Lehrs, Richard Meyer, Hermann von Baravalle, Eugen Kolisko. Karl Schubert, Rudolf Kayser and Helga Biedermann.

the opportunity to meet the owner of the Waldorf Astoria Cigarette Factory and founder of the school. Steiner also visited often, as did the teachers of the school and poets such as Hermann Hesse.

I started this chapter with the question: "Where is Widukind?" And now we see a young man sitting at table with Emil Molt, just past childhood, who joined the Waldorf school completely at his own initiative, precisely at the time when Walter Johannes Stein was going to tell the story about Widukind in his class.

Rudolf Grosse told this story also, including the impression it made on him. Of course he did not know that the story went on when his teacher, Walter Johannes Stein, told it to Steiner, who then explained why it made such an impression on the class: "No wonder; they were the Saxons who were there."

Rudolf Grosse pointed the way to Widukind. He sat at table with Emil Molt and felt born anew. Old karma received a future in the light of a new pedagogy born from the true spirit of the time.

The Destruction of the Irminsul (Fresco from 1848)

12

ALEXANDER STRAKOSCH AND PAULINUS OF AQUILEIA

A SOURCE FOR THE SUBJECT THE ART OF LIFE

Alexander Strakosch was born on August 23, 1879. He became a teacher at the first Waldorf school in Stuttgart in 1920. But he had already attended the training course Rudolf Steiner had given in September 1919 before the school opened. He was not there during the first year, but was soon asked to accompany a class as class teacher, a task he took on as a matter of course as if he had never done anything else in his life. The pupils received great insight from him into their own time, something they were longing for. One can say that already then Strakosch was teaching the subject The Art of Life, which later became his most important task. His colleague Herbert Hahn called Strakosch the founder of this subject.

Alexander Strakosch had known Steiner since 1908. His wife, Maria Giesler, and he heard Steiner for the first time in Berlin when he gave a lecture on the sun, moon and stars. Maria was an artist and had been taught by Kandinsky. Their connection with anthroposophy also became a personal friendship with Steiner for this couple.

Until his move to the Waldorf school, Alexander Strakosch worked as a signal engineer for the Austrian railways. He and Maria lived for a long time in Trieste which then still belonged to the Austrian Habsburg Empire. They started meeting on a personal basis when Rudolf and Marie Steiner were on vacation in this area in the years before World War I. Strakosch wrote about this with much love in his autobiography in the chapters about 'Rudolf Steiner on the Adriatic Coast' and 'Aquileia.' Alexander Strakosch wrote in his memoirs the following about Aquileia:

Like enormous walls, the Carinthian Alps rise up out of the plain of Friuli. With snow-covered heads they look down upon the blossoming plain at their feet, which stretches in its green fertility to the Adriatic Sea. A few miles west of where the river Isonzo winds its way through the Karst area and in many branches flows into the sea, there is a small town. The tall steeple of a basilica rises above the low rooflines of the houses. The town is surrounded by a plain that nourishes vineyards, mulberry trees, grain, corn and rice. But for the immense church, no one would ever suspect that there had been a large city here in antiquity and in the Middle Ages.

It was one of the nine principal cities in the empire and was after Rome the most important place for the spread of Christianity. The museum and its gardens exhibit not only sculptures and objects from ancient Roman times, but also objects and art from the time of beginning Christianity. It is said that the apostle Mark preached here. A great many old mystery cults and also Celtic customs were preserved here and the arts were cultivated. Aquileia was a center of the art of glassblowing.

It is impossible to give a brief description of Aquileia's significance for early Christian culture. Its patriarch was, after the pope, one of the most important personalities in the development of Christianity. In 1911 I had the good fortune of visiting this place together with Rudolf Steiner and some other people close to him.[38]

Alexander Strakosch

Alexander Strakosch then describes how he encountered this old culture together with Steiner. It is striking that he devotes several chapters of his memoirs to this visit. He gives an extensive description of the art of glassblowing and the coloring of the glass. It is as if he found part of his own being there.

Let us now switch over to the teachers at the Court School of Charlemagne. There we meet an important personality and friend of Alcuin, Paulinus of Aquileia. This Paulinus was the patriarch of Aquileia, and in the time he was working at the Court School Alcuin called him Timothy after St. Paul's favorite pupil. Alcuin continued to write to him with much warmth, also after Paulinus had been named patriarch of Aquileia:

> Do not forget the name of your Alcuin in your prayers, especially when you consecrate the elements of bread and wine into the substance of the most holy Body and Blood of Christ. I have long been expecting those relics you promised me, of the True Cross and others.

Here speaks the connection both men have with the Christ power that works down into earthly substance. In the Grail mysteries a path was taught to take this transforming Christ power into one's own being. The power of the Holy Cross had an important place in this. In the Grail mysteries the pupils, who in Carolingian time had the name Parsifal, oriented themselves meditatively to the cross. Steiner said the following about this:

> And Parsifal saw that purification was not enough, that he must nail his lower self on the black cross and live according to the life of Christ so that the red roses could blossom. After this Parsifal went into solitude and let the symbols work within him day and night. With time, the symbols grew pale, but a seed had sprung from them. In his solitude he looked around, he looked forward and backward, above and below, right and left—and he felt a great unity, the great enveloper. He felt strong currents flowing into him from all sides and he felt them working together towards a point within and that this point is part of the great enveloper.[39]

The two friends seem to have found each other in their striving in these Grail mysteries. The theme of the Holy Cross is not just an outer motif but a real indication of the path of their inner development.

This building up and caring for the inner cross also has an important place in Waldorf pedagogy. In the lower school we give much attention to orientation and movement exercises which bring to consciousness front and back, above and below, left and right. This is more explicitly practiced in eurythmy and Bothmer gymnastics. We could even say that this striving forms the basis of the subject The

Art of Life that pervades all of Waldorf pedagogy; as a subject, The Art of Life can lay the foundation for a true art of life in later years. An ability to relate to the surroundings out of the spatial directions can then grow into a social capacity to deal in freedom with life situations. The disposition for the subject The Art of Life, as it was developed by Alexander Strakosch as pioneer in the Waldorf school, encompasses metamorphosed elements of the medieval Grail mysteries.

Both Alcuin and Paulinus witnessed the building of the church (*Dom*) in Aachen. Charlemagne had ordered columns from early Christian churches in Ravenna, Italy, to give them a place in the design for his Christian temple. Alcuin must surely have advised Charles, for he brought building experience from York where he had been the leader of the famous monastery school for many years (see chapter 5). Paulinus was also connected with the building impulse that lived at the court of Charlemagne. As one of the carrying teachers of the school, he made contributions to the form of the church as 'Temple of Sophia, Heavenly Wisdom,' as Alcuin called it.

Just as Alcuin had a connection in friendship and striving with Paulinus, there was also a special connection between Karl Stockmeyer and Alexander Strakosch that even went back to a time before they met at the first Waldorf school. They had both taken up the construction of the first Goetheanum as 'House of the Word,' but also as 'Temple of Wisdom' with great strength, and had supported it with their own designs.

Thus Karl Stockmeyer made a small model of a temple with two times seven columns as a kernel for the building of the first Goetheanum. Alexander Strakosch worked on the problem of the double domes. This was not yet part of Karl Stockmeyer's model of 1909, since the space he designed had the form of an ellipse. In 1911 Strakosch went a step further.

> At that time I worked on plans for a building that our friends in
> Munich wanted to build as a center for activities and as the future
> School of Spiritual Science. At that time Rudolf Steiner visited us
> in our modest home in Bled [now in Slovenia], and I accompanied
> him when he left. For some time we were sitting at the foot of a
> great boulder that had an inscription that the poet Anastasius Grün
> liked to sit here to look out over the lake and the mountains. There
> I asked Rudolf Steiner for more detailed indications for the ground
> plan of the building.

He only said: "You should take two circles that penetrate into each other." I asked about the diameters of those two circles and how deeply they should penetrate each other. "You would have to investigate that," was the answer. At my next visit I brought a design with me for the two domes adapted to the situation in Munich. (The building in Dornach was made with slightly different proportions.) I arrived at the height of the domes on the basis of a pentagondodecahedron that had a particular relationship with the ground plan. This solution clearly interested Rudolf Steiner. At another occasion he said: "The dodecahedron, that is the human being."[40]

The ceilings of both spaces were designed as half domes. The bigger space was projected around the dodecahedron, the smaller one inside it.

Both Alexander Strakosch and Karl Stockmeyer were again and again stimulated by Steiner to work with him on the design of the first Goetheanum. This even went to the point that one day Steiner gave a lecture on the Goetheanum that was totally oriented on the mathematical construction aspect. No one understood why Steiner did this because something else had been announced beforehand, until Carl Unger realized that Alexander Strakosch was in the room.[41]

The fact that the lecture was really meant for Strakosch became clear years later when Steiner said in a meeting with teachers: "And now Mr. Strakosch will show us in his enthusiastic way how we can explain the geometric forms we discussed years ago in Dornach to fourteen-year olds." He referred to the event described above that had happened five years earlier!

Just as Alcuin found a kindred spirit in Paulinus in his work at the Court School of Charlemagne, this was also the case between Stockmeyer and Strakosch on their path toward the foundation of the first Waldorf school.

What did the subject The Art of Life (*Lebenskunde*) really mean to Alexander Strakosch? When he became a Waldorf teacher in 1920, Strakosch was asked by Steiner to give two lectures at the first conference of the School of Spiritual Science in Dornach on the subject Signaling in its Cultural-Historical Significance. This was a big surprise for him. People even quipped that he had not yet let go of his technological past. But then he gave his lectures and began by talking about the signaling fires with which the Greeks announced the fall of Troy throughout their country. He ended with the transmission of signals by modern railways.

He described how such changes express changes in consciousness in the course of human history. He also developed the subject of The Art of Life on the basis of technology, but in the process awakened interest in the spiritual evolution of humanity. He wrote about his own experiences:

> In ancient times people experienced the presence of a creative spirit in all of creation. The human being was formed as a kind of mirror image, but in the course of time became more and more independent. In our time we are standing at the beginning of an era in which the newly independent human spirit connects itself in a new way with the creative world spirit by its autonomous collaboration and co-creation. When this conception lives in the soul of the teacher, (s)he becomes able to speak about nature and culture with living force. The meaning of world evolution will resound in their lessons as a living element without being put into actual words. In this way forces can sprout in the souls of the pupils that are able to maintain life in the face of technology.[42]

The Art of Life is a very broad theme in education. There are sources teachers can use for it. One such source can be the effort to place oneself in the flow of the year. At the beginning of the day in a Waldorf school the teachers come together and read the verse of the week from the *Calendar of the Soul* by Rudolf Steiner. Steiner wrote these verses in Portorose on the Adriatic Sea when he and Alexander Strakosch were visiting Aquileia. Strakosch witnessed the origin of this creative process which would be so important for Waldorf schools. In the atmosphere of old Aquileia, Steiner and Alexander Strakosch found each other and renewed old karma for new deeds in the field of pedagogy and the art of life.

Strakosch died on February 5, 1958, in Dornach after completing a course on temple building from the temple of Solomon to the Goetheanum. When we want to try and give new form to the subject of The Art of Life in our own Waldorf schools we may draw inspiration from his work and striving.

1 3

THE POET NOTKER AND
THEMES IN THE LIFE OF ERNST UEHLI

*T*he title of this chapter points to two figures who came into the world a thousand years apart. Notker is not a well-known name. And Ernst Uehli (1875–1959) belonged to the first Waldorf teachers and authored many books. He also had an important part in the development of the religious instruction in the school, and also of the Children's Service. Despite the long interval, a biographical comparison will prove to be fruitful in order to understand the spiritual impulse of these two personalities.

The poet Notker was also called Notker the Stammerer or Notker Balbulus. As he explained himself, he owed this epithet to his teeth because they were the cause of a handicap in his speech. He is known especially for the hymns he wrote. His being fully unfolded in the element of music. His poems, as well as his biography of Charlemagne radiate great lyrical power. His name and his being are strongly connected with the monastery of St. Gall in today's St. Gallen, Switzerland.

It is presumed that Notker was born around 840. In the 13th century the village of Elgg, east of Winterthur in the canton of Zurich, Switzerland, was considered to be his birthplace. His brother Othere owned rich possessions in Thurgau.

Ernst Uehli was born in a beautiful house in Andelfingen, Switzerland, close to the wooden bridge over the river Thur, just north of Winterthur. No one could then predict that in his forty-fourth year this boy would become one of the carrying personalities of the first Waldorf school in Stuttgart. Before this happened in 1920, he was to follow a path which seems to have an inner relationship with the life of the poet Notker.

Ernst Uehli

We find Notker already at a young age in the monastery of St. Gall. It seems that his father had died early, and during the first years of his life, he was brought up by his uncle Adalbert, an old warrior, who went with Charlemagne on his campaigns against the Saxons. This old knight must have told the boy many stories about Charlemagne and his paladins. These stories must surely have laid the foundation for his later biography of the Frankish emperor.

Notker (From an 11th century anonymous manuscript)

According to Wolfram von der Steinen, who published a powerful work about Notker in 1948, the boy was probably taken to the monastery when he was six. One of the leading monks was a son of the then seventy-year-old uncle and knight. This monk, Werinbert was his name, accompanied the child and gave him the opportunity to study the Seven Liberal Arts.

One single incident from his school years has been handed down by tradition. Once he studied a book from the nearby monastery of Reichenau, which contained the Old Testament book of Ezra. The Persian king Darius is listening to three of his guards arguing about who is the strongest on earth. The first says: wine; the second: the emperor; and the third first mentions women but then changes his mind and says: truth. They all make a speech and, in the end, the third one wins. When Notker read this he indignantly put the book away. The story shows the strict moral earnestness of the youth.

Notker did not travel much in his long life. We almost always find him around Lake Constance and even there mostly within the walls of the monastery of St. Gall. He studied, wrote and sang. But most of all he was the favorite teacher of many pupils. Tradition relates that they longed to be with their teacher as often as possible to study under his guidance. From his side, Notker also closely identified with his pupils, even when their ways gave him cause for concern. This was the case with the brothers Waldo and Salomo van Freising who wrote to Notker:

O you blessed one, where are you, o master? O what is the matter
and why do you not answer me? Why do you appear so seldom
and are you so distant? We implore you, come at last! And bestow
your instruction on us more often! May the Lord give you thanks
hundredfold. Our quills call you back; lamb skin, the golden fleece,
wish to see you.[43]

Notker replied as follows:

From the Book of Nature I want to tell you something, so that you
will know and learn how faithful I have been to you as your friend.
As long as white down envelops the raven young, the parents—
unjustly it seems—do not care for the chicks. Only when the black
feathers begin to cover them do they recognize their own young
and begin to feed them.[44]

Notker seems to refer to the black habit of the Benedictine monks, but it could
also have a deeper meaning.

In the ancient Persian path of initiation, which was later brought to Europe
by Roman soldiers, the developmental stage of the Raven was the first step of
inner growth. In the rest of his reply Notker called on his pupils not to let go
of the inner path of development. He also used the image of the eagle which
abandons its young if they are not able to direct their just-opened eyes to the
sun. The picture of the eagle always represents St John the Evangelist. In this way
Notker made a direct connection between the pre-Christian initiation of Mithras
with the Christian initiation described in the Gospel of St. John. Both paths
encompassed seven stages.

Besides his pupils, Notker had in St. Gallen two trusted friends, Ratpert and
Tutilo.

Two hours after midnight, after singing the Lauds, the three men
met in the scriptorium where they spent the time doing work
together and exchanging idea while others were sleeping. Tutilo was
by nature a real artist. He painted and wrote poems. He sang and
played all instruments like a master. He worked gold and carved
ivory. But at the same time he was able to chase robbers away with
a gnarled oak branch he quickly picked up from the ground.

The monastery in St. Gallen still owns two ivory carvings by Tutilo. Embedded in silver and decorated with precious stones, these form the cover of a copy of the gospels. Notker's other friend, Ratpert, was more strict; he used only two pairs of shoes per year. This peculiarity is used to illustrate how rarely he came out of the monastery. He was a benevolent and sharp teacher but called traveling a form of death, differently from Tutilo who loved to travel. With great precision Ratpert worked out the rights of the community of the monastery.

Ernst also lost his father at a young age. This caused him deep suffering. In his autobiographical sketch he wrote the touching words: "Father! Father! Never did the longing for my father disappear after he left us."

In 1896 he took a job with the customs authority in St. Gallen. He was then twenty-one years old. It was not easy work for him. As customs official he had to keep book of incoming and outgoing goods. Still, he also described the wealth that went by him. St. Gallen imported a lot of textiles in those days to supply its many clothing and embroidery workshops. Thus Ernst had to evaluate things like raw cotton from Manchester, bleached linen from Belfast, and silk from China. Everything had to be judged not on its own value but purely by weight. It is clear that he disliked that.

In St. Gallen he joined the Chamber of Commerce and made there two friends for life, together with whom he immersed himself in literature. They started a small literary circle where they read dramas and lyrical poems, especially the poems of Christian Morgenstern. In that period Ernst also experienced a performance of *Lohengrin* by Richard Wagner, which became the beginning of a lifelong relationship with the work of this magician-composer. After the performance he could not sleep all night. The appearance of the swan knight and his provenance kept him awake. "My inner being was touched by the secret of the Grail." Later Ernst would leave an indelible impression on his pupils, as shown by the following poem by Erika Belte:

To the Teacher

When I see your countenance,
Warmly bathed in your dear look,
I sense the field of stars around you
And it is as if I see far back.
Somewhere, before I came here,

The same image cast a spell on me.
Wordless do I feel your being
Kindred to my inmost soul.
The same footsteps I hear sound,
The same star tone reminding me of home;
But while I am still walking, you are bounding,
What I would be, you already are.[45]

He knew how to awaken enthusiasm for learning in his pupils.

In Ernst Uehli we had a teacher who in his inclinations, talent
and destiny seemed to be predestined for teaching art history in
the Waldorf school. …The enthusiasm of the children for their art
history classes created in the parents the desire to have something
similar. Thus Ernst Uehli gave a number of art presentations with
slides on Friday evenings for parents and older students. Many
people, including factory workers, came to these evenings. They
experienced the great, vivifying creative power of the great art works
of humanity.[46]

Notker became known especially as a poet of hymns and sequences. Wolfram von der Steinen, whom we mentioned already, collected theses hymns into a book. They follow the course of the year: Easter, Ascension and Whitsun form the Easter season. From Christmas to Candlemas the hymns focus on Mary. Between Michaelmas and Christmas the great saints are celebrated. These hymns have great spiritual power and are dedicated to Liutward of Vercelli, counselor to Charles III (the Fat). Liutward was educated in Reichenau. He was also the protector of the monastery of St. Gall in St. Gallen which Charles III visited in 883.

The Book of Hymns of Notker opens with a number of verses dedicated to Liutward of Vercelli. The book, which Notker himself called a small and pitiful little thing, appeared in 884. Between the Easter hymns and those for Christmas, Notker again placed eight hexameters dedicated to Liutward. After Candlemas we enter the 'narrow path' of the Passion. Lent transitions to the Crucifixion and the descent of Christ into the underworld. In the eight hexameters Notker conceives of the destiny of Christ as Son of God and the destiny of humanity as a unity. He concludes with the words: "You will find bliss in the king who was crucified here."

Here shimmers the deep Christian conviction that with Christ His true disciple is also "crucified for the world" (Galatians 6–14).

As we have seen, Notker had a close relationship with Liutward; for this reason he also included a hymn to Eusebius, who was the first bishop of Vercelli in the 4th century. As Walter Johannes Stein showed in his book *The Ninth Century*, this Liutward can be connected with the historical Parsifal. In his hymns to the saints Notker connects the earth with the stars. This is the theme of Grail Christianity. His friend Ratpert also wrote of St. Gall: "Every year we celebrate, O Holy God, the festive day on which father Gallus ascended from the earth to the stars."

From the letter to Liutward at the beginning of the *Book of Hymns* we learn that he was the leader of the monastery of Columbanus in Bobbio (Italy). And St. Gall or Gallus was the most trusted pupil of Columbanus! The Irish-Celtic oriented monastery of St. Gall was a true source of Grail Christianity in the 9th century, for the folk spirit of the Celts became the protective spirit of esoteric Grail Christianity.

It was in St. Gallen that Ernst Uehli's spiritual awakening took place. He read much literature during his work and acquired his own library. A number of different influences worked on him. He read all of Conrad Ferdinand Meyer's works in his midday breaks. His experiences with a man who had a family led him to abstain from alcohol. That which he imagined as a kind of round table assemblage was still eluding him. The painter Böcklin had a powerful attraction for him.

It is interesting that both Böcklin and Meyer are described by Rudolf Steiner in his karma lectures of 1924. Both of them have a karma that is related to the Anglo-Saxon world, Böcklin as one of King Arthur's knights and Meyer as a priest from Ravenna in the retinue of St. Augustine of Canterbury who tried to convert the Saxons in England in the 6th century. On April 23, 1924, Steiner said about Meyer that he was sent from Italy to England by Pope Gregory, that in him a kind of double nature was living, and that he was an enthusiastic devotee of the art of mosaics.

Later Ernst Uehli was to publish a magnificent book on the mosaics in Ravenna. It must have touched him deeply to have heard Steiner speak about this author whose work he had read with such dedication in his twenties. The first seed for another book also dates back to his time in St. Gallen. He came to know the *Ring of the Nibelungen* by Richard Wagner. His deep impression gave him the impulse to write a book on Wagner and his work. The book was reprinted many times. In 1926 Uehli's book on Norse mythology appeared.

Hidden under the cover of his official desk he also read Wolfram von Eschenbach's *Parsifal* and also *Tristan* by Gottfried von Strassburg. Again we see the connection of the knight of King Arthur, Grail King and the world of the Germanic gods.

In September 1906 Ernst Uehli traveled to Bregenz on Lake Constance, the city where Columbanus and Gallus had separated long before. He climbed the Pfänder Mountain. For hours he drank in the panorama of Lake Constance stretched out below him. The next morning he felt as born anew.

Christmas time in 1908 brought a second step in his inner development. Ernst described his experience as follows:

> Ever since my childhood the great feast days of Christmas and
> Easter were like milestones for me in the course of the year. With
> a powerful life force they lifted me out of everyday existence. It
> was often difficult for me to come back to daily life again. As often
> as possible I spent Christmas with my mother at her house. But
> Christmas 1908 developed in such a way that I stayed in Zurich
> completely alone … A mood enveloped me that came from sleep
> and took me back into the world of sleep again. This mood was like
> a still, radiant white splendor. But it was not a mood of nature. The
> substance of which it was woven did not have to do with the senses,
> but it was born out of the soul itself.

When we follow Ernst Uehli in his inner journey on his hike up the mountain near Bregenz and in this lily-white Christmas experience, we unwittingly think of the path through life of Parsifal. Steiner described this path in his lectures of August 1909 (see Esoteric Lessons 1904–1909, GA 266/1). The path first leads up the mountain where the pupil experiences himself in space as a point in the center of a threefold cross formed by the spatial directions. Next he sees himself in the image of the white lily. He expels everything evil and lowly out of himself. He experiences the earth as a great, pure plant being.

That was the second stage of the Parsifal initiation Ernst Uehli went through. Then followed the Easter experience of 1909:

I spent the two Easter days in a small mountain village. A pretty
rocky road went up from the station. It was Easter morning. Down
below I was looking over the silver reflecting surface of a mountain
lake. The sun spread its golden rays over the mountain tops and
snowy fields of the Glanner Alps. I slowed my pace and sat down
on a boulder. The sound of my footsteps seemed improper in the
magic of this festive morning. The mood of Good Friday was still
living in full strength in my soul. Still solitude enveloped the word
that was sensed but not spoken. What I then experienced was
no nature impression; it was a soul image that came to me from
outside. The word that was not formed but which I had sensed
changed into an image, and I knew with the certainty with which
one knows that the sun has risen, that I had received a sign, a
message from the Grail.

This third experience is like that of the Rose on the Parsifal path as described
by Steiner:

In the deep solitude in which he stood, he looked around. He
looked forward and backward, up and down, right and left. And
he felt the great unity in everything. He felt the great enveloper,
the all-encompassing one. And he felt how the all-encompassing
one sent him forces from all sides, and he experienced himself as a
point, the middle point, the center of these forces.[47]

It is as if these three experiences awakened in Uehli the forces of a Grail
initiation he had gone through in the 9th century, and that this initiation repeated
itself spontaneously during his life in the 20th century. The awakening power
originated from anthroposophy which Ernst Uehli had encountered in Steiner
in 1905 and which had occupied him intensively ever since. During these years
he lived deeply with the question of Atlantis, a theme that must also have lived
among the Irish-oriented Grail Christians of St. Gallen. Later Uehli was to write
an extensive book about Atlantis and art during the Ice Age.

The three stages experienced between 1906 and 1909 are preparations for his
later task as teacher of religion and art history at the Waldorf school. Life itself
took him onto a path of initiation that is related to the Grail. Anthroposophy is

"the science of the Grail," said Steiner. And it was Steiner who gave the impetus for this entire process of Grail initiation. Uehli had these experiences after he heard Steiner speak in St. Gallen on September 8, 1905, about our planetary system. "Every sentence, every thought made a deep impression on me," said Uehli later. A few months earlier he had reached his thirtieth year!

Around the year 1000, Eckehart IV wrote the following about Notker: "As the Spirit animates him Notker creates his hymns. He celebrates in song what was proclaimed to Abraham, as well as the festivals in the course of the year. Wondrous was the dew that flowed from his mouth. ..."

The same author from St. Gallen wrote an epitaph for him: "On April 6, the melodious voice of Notker fell silent. He celebrated in song how the uncreated was incarnated, and he proclaimed the sevenfold breath of the Holy Spirit. His mighty intervals will assure this man, so exceptional in the art of singing, a place in heaven."

The epitaph on his grave reads as follows: "Here, in this grave, rests the fame of his fatherland, the teacher of wisdom Notker, a mortal man. On April 6 he left his body and, received with song, entered heaven."

In 1937 Ernst Uehli returned to Switzerland after living in Germany for twenty-five years. Since 1920 he had been connected with the Waldorf school in Stuttgart as art history and religion teacher. He was one of the few non-priests who had attended the founding of the Christian Community by Steiner. He led the Sunday Service for Children at the school and had also taken part in the courses Steiner gave for the priests. After he left Germany at age 63, he wrote two books about Egyptian and Greek cultural history after which he concluded his work with a short book about "Karma Order and Rights Order." It is as if we hear him speak once again, in the spirit, with Notker's friend Ratpert.

Notker and Ernst Uehli, both connected with St. Gallen, were in search of the Grail. In Liutward of Vercelli Notker found an envoy of the Grail; Ernst Uehli found his way to the modern Grail mysteries in his encounter with Steiner. He became a much loved teacher, just like Notker. Notker sang, Uehli spoke in pictures. Across the stream of a thousand years of time they were connected in their search for the Grail. Their journey guided them to fruitful cultural impulses as teachers and authors filled with art.

1 4

Parsifal and the Task of the Waldorf School Movement – 1

*T*he epic of Parsifal is part of the curriculum of the eleventh grade in the Waldorf schools. Parsifal's adventures, as related by the text, can lead to discussions with the students of many themes in human life. In the beginning, his path is one of deep unconsciousness. When the young knight wakes up from this dull condition he finds himself in a state of great inner doubt. In the end he finds the way out of this doubt toward the inner tranquility of *saelde* (inner peace).

Rudolf Steiner pointed out that Parsifal was the first one to travel the path to the consciousness soul:

> In the whole picture drawn of Parsifal, if rightly understood, we
> can find all the different methods of training the consciousness
> soul which are necessary to evoke from it the right effects, so that
> the person can gain control of the forces which whirl in confusion
> and strive against one another in the intellectual or mind soul.
> The more present-day man looks into himself and tries to exercise
> honest self-knowledge, the more he will find how conflict is raging
> in his soul; it is a conflict within the intellectual or mind soul.[48]

This battle is pointed out to the students when, accompanied by their teacher, they discuss Parsifal and learn how the conflict relates to their own lives. In order to enter fully into the drama of this biography, it is important that we realize that Parsifal was a real historical personality.

When Walter Johannes Stein gave his first Parsifal block, Steiner pointed out to him and the students that Parsifal lived eleven generations before the story was told. Wolfram von Eschenbach expressed this: "Alas that we do not now have her like even to the eleventh generation!"[49] Counting back together at the rate of thirty years per generation, they arrive at the year 870. The 9th century is the time when the real Parsifal can be found. But we also have to realize that there were many Parsifals, for the name Parsifal indicated a degree of initiation in the Christian mysteries of the Middle Ages.

The historical Parsifal described by Wolfram von Eschenbach is the pioneer on the path of development mentioned above. Walter Johannes Stein went on a search for this historical Parsifal and found him in the figure of Liutward of Vercelli. He describes his search in his book *The Ninth Century*. Liutward was a counselor to Charles the Fat and his wife Richardis. Stein points out that a number of old sources have more to say about this Liutward. Chapter 14 contains more detailed information about the historical Parsifal gleaned from these old sources.

The reason for giving attention to the historical Parsifal in a contemplation on the karma of the Waldorf school movement is the expectation that this same individuality will now, at the beginning of the 21st century, be able to have a new essential influence on the development of human culture. Steiner pointed out that in the historical Parsifal we can recognize the same individuality that was the founder of the Christian stream of Manichaeism in the 3rd century AD. In an incarnation prior to that he was the Young Man of Nain, and received initiation by Christ Himself. In the Gospel of St. Luke this initiation is described as a raising from the dead (Luke 7:11–17).

And this young man is also the same as the Youth of Sais about whom the German poet Friedrich Schiller wrote a moving poem. Tradition relates that this youth approached the statue of Isis in the temple of Sais before being fully prepared. He removed the veils that enveloped the statue. Under the statue was the inscription: "No mortal may lift my veil. I am who was and is and is to be!" A contemporary of Schiller, Goalies, replied to this poem with the words: "If no mortal may lift the veils in Sais, we are called to become immortal. With these words Novalis calls on us to achieve a new Christian initiation."

The development of a new Christian path of initiation is the central theme in the successive lives of the Parsifal individuality. This path of initiation leads right through the middle of life. One way of rendering the meaning of the name Parsifal is 'straight through the middle.' This also indicates finding the 'middle way.' This striving has to do with the recognition of evil as the loss of the middle between hardening and dissolving, between too much and too little, too short and too long.

And this brings us back to the daily lesson practice and intercourse with the children where we are constantly faced with the question of too much or too little, too short or too long. The different subjects provide us with exercises here, especially music. We can also see the historical Liutward-Parsifal as a seeker for the middle. For that reason he was often not understood and was even attacked and accused of treason. In historical tradition such accusations are mentioned frequently. I have tried to find the underlying motives for these accusations.

The search for the middle is a theme that in our time is more relevant than ever before. Mighty spiritual beings are lurking in the extremes. We know them by the names of Lucifer and Ahriman. Through them works another, even more powerful, anti-Christian being often called the Antichrist. Following occult Jewish teaching, Steiner also called this being Sorath. There where the middle is lost Sorath seeks entry into the human being and attempts to make him his possession. In this battle for the middle, the Parsifal individuality wants to form the vanguard. Steiner was once asked when Parsifal would be born again. His replies speak for themselves, and gave me the impetus for this contemplation:

> Mani will not incarnate during this [20th] century, but intends to do so in the next century provided he can find a suitable body. The ordinary kind of education would not provide any possibility for Mani to develop; only Waldorf education would do so. If the right conditions are provided he will appear as a teacher of humankind and take up leadership in matters of art and religion. He will act from the power of the Grail mysteries, and he will encourage humankind to decide for themselves even about good and evil.[50]

> Beginning in our time we are moving to a future cultural era in which Mani [Parsifal] will be a leader and will introduce Christian principles applied in a practical way in social life.[51]

> The Threefold Social Order of Rudolf Steiner is particularly a preparatory work to bring about a human incarnation of Manes. …He said that Manes could not yet find a suitable body, that all the forces he would be able to bring to an incarnation would be destroyed by modern education. Therefore he said that the need was that the Waldorf school education be manifested and that

the Threefold Social Order be manifested. …By karma, Manes' incarnation would be due by the end of the [20th] century.

Whether this will be possible I do not know, but if the Threefold Order and Waldorf education are established he could incarnate again. Such an incarnation would bring about a complete change of trend in history. [52]

These three quotations show the importance Steiner attached to Waldorf pedagogy. I leave it to the reader to find the characteristics Steiner meant to indicate, that enable Waldorf pedagogy to be a portal to the world for this Christian initiate. The search for the middle between extremes could be a key here. The entire course *Study of Man* by Rudolf Steiner carries the sign of the search for the middle. In the following chapters we will turn to the historical Parsifal and become part of his trials and adventures.

15

Parsifal and the Task of the Waldorf School Movement – 2

Chapter 13 contains a discussion of the development of a new Christian path of initiation. The first person to tread this path was the individuality called Parsifal we encounter in Wolfram von Eschenbach's epic. In the beginning of our century this individuality might incarnate again and become a leader of humanity in the arts and religion. The kind of education he will need as a young person in order to retain his forces must be based on the middle. We now turn to the historical Parsifal to take part in his trials and adventures.

Charles III, 'the Fat' (839–888), had a counselor he trusted with his whole heart. His name was Liutward of Vercelli (a town between Milan and Turin, Italy). Liutward possessed exceptional books. Besides Latin he probably also knew Greek. We may cautiously conclude this from the following communication in the Annals of St. Gallen where Notker and the way in which he related to Liutward are described as follows:

> We will now write down without second thoughts what remains
> to be said about Notker. We do not doubt for a moment that he
> is a chosen chalice into which the Holy Spirit is descended. At the
> end of his life a great sorrow befell him that cut him to the heart.
> Liutward of Vercelli had lent him a Greek copy of the canonical
> Letters of the Apostles and St. Paul. With great pains and effort
> Notker had copied these.

His distress was caused by the fact that this work, which he had written with great labor, was stolen from him and later retrieved all crumpled up.

With regard to Liutward we can learn from this description that he had mastered the Greek language. He probably had a connection with Irish Christians since those were the ones who were able to translate Greek texts into good Latin. One of them was a contemporary of Liutward, John Scotus Eriugena. The letters of St. Paul that Notker had borrowed from Liutward contain much that relates to Grail Christianity. In the 13th century Thomas Aquinas wrote an extensive commentary on these letters. Walter Johannes Stein described their Grail content based on Thomas' commentary. The theme of the letters is 'Not I but Christ in me.' The human soul becomes the chalice in which the Christ substance is taken up, the Chalice of the Holy Grail.

Liutward went the 'path through the valley' to 'sanctify' the soul. In the 9th century this inner way was viewed as the search for the Holy Grail. Studying the Greek version of the letters of St. Paul had a stimulating effect on this way. The Greek language is more poetical and less intellectual than Latin.

Liutward went a path of trials. This is a confirmation of the other side of the path the Grail seeker travels on his way. Every Grail seeker was called a 'Parsifal' in the Middle Ages. This term indicates a grade of inner development. 'Parsifal' then meant the 'passage through the valley' during which one had to undergo severe trials caused by one's own guilt. And then one had to face one's guilt as folly. That is why the young knight, who was later to go the Parsifal path, was called a 'fool.'

After folly came the stage in which one was a 'Red Knight.' The red knight lives in the force of the blood and egoism. Our Liutward showed these aspects on his Parsifal path. He was accused of being power hungry in his high office. The story in the *Annales Fuldenses*[53] for the year 882 includes the following:

> When the emperor Charles learned of the death of his brother
> [Louis the Younger], he traveled from Italy to Bavaria. There he met
> with the noblemen who had served his brother and now recognized
> Charles as their supreme lord. Next he deliberated with his subjects,
> who had come to Worms from everywhere, how they could chase
> the Norsemen from the empire. After they had determined the time
> by which a large army would come together, innumerable forces
> assembled from all provinces; these would certainly have struck fear
> in the heart of any enemy if their leaders had been united. There
> were Franks, Norics,[54] Alemanians,[55] Thuringians,[56] and Saxons.[57]
> They made a united front to fight the enemy. When they reached
> their destination they surrounded the fortress of the Norsemen at
> Elsloo in Limburg [now in the south of The Netherlands].

When the stronghold had almost fallen, and the people inside
were convinced they would not escape death, one of the emperor's
counselors, a false bishop named Liutward, went together with
double-faced count Wicbert to the emperor, unbeknownst to the
other counselors who had already served the emperor's father.
Bribed with money they convinced the emperor not to destroy the
enemy, and introduced the leader of the enemy to him. Just like
Ahab, the emperor received him as a friend, and after hostages had
been exchanged the peace was signed.

Next is related how the Norsemen devised a ruse and how they trapped part of
the imperial army inside the castle of Elsloo. But Charles stayed with his decision:
he had Gottfried baptized and appointed him as co-ruler. It is quite conceivable
that, in an era in which blood-feud was the rule, this deed of Liutward bred ill will
in the retinue of the emperor. That he would have been bribed seems improbable.
They probably could not figure out any other reason for the way he had acted.

Precisely from this description we can see that in Liutward we have to do with
a Christian initiate. He transformed the vendetta as given in the Old Testament
into forgiveness and Christian love. The name Ahab creates a conspicuous
relationship with the Old Testament.

Liutward, by the way, was also accused of being a false bishop. Since the 8th
century the term 'false bishop' was used by the Church of Rome for Irish-Celtic
bishops who did not submit to the jurisdiction of Rome. There are letters from St.
Boniface in which he used the same term for a number of contemporaries. Pope
Zacharias replied around 742 to a letter from St. Boniface as follows: "The false
priests, however, of which you inform me as a brother that you have encountered
more than Catholics, the followers of the false doctrine who purport to be
priests and bishops without ever having been ordained by catholic bishops…"[58]
This letter certainly makes clear what was meant with the term 'false bishops.'
Liutward, however, had no need to be concerned about these accusations; he just
kept on working in 882.

The threat of the Norsemen was still there. Although in the end they pulled
back with their booty of gold and silver, the annals have this to say for the same
year 882: "The Norsemen burned down the market town with the Frisian name of
Deventer and in doing so killed many people." (*Annales Fuldenses*). It is a question
whether Liutward's act vis-à-vis the Norsemen had been the right thing to do.

We do read though that the converted Norse leader Gottfried remained faithful to the emperor. This is what the annals say about him for the year 883: "The Norseman Gottfried, who had himself baptized in the spring, entered into an alliance with Hugh, son of Lothar, and married his sister."

And yet, the Norsemen kept coming. In this year came "the Norsemen. They sailed up the Rhine and put the villages and towns that had only just recovered to the torch. They captured a lot of booty." And for 884: "The Norsemen tried to invade Saxony. On Candlemas [February 2] the emperor called an assembly of his subjects in Colmar [Alsace, France], and from there he issued commands to bishops, abbots and counts to defend the various parts of the empire."

It is interesting that this happened in Colmar in Alsace, because the empress Richardis liked to come to Alsace and had founded a cloister in Andlau, north of Colmar, on the spot which, tradition says, a she-bear had indicated to her. Here Liutward was not only counselor to the emperor, but also the spiritual advisor of the empress. This is pictured on the west portal of the church in Andlau.

Ever since the arrival of Columbanus and his companions, Irish-Celtic Christianity was living on in many personalities in Alsace. Again and again Irish and Anglo-Saxon monks traveled to Alsace. Niedermünster and Mount Odile were spiritual centers ever since the beginning of the 8th century. The founding of the cloister in Andlau by Richard was part of this stream. The assembly in Colmar should also be viewed in this light.

In subsequent years the noblemen tried a different approach to discredit Liutward in the eyes of the emperor. The *Annales Fuldenses* relate the following for 887:

> For he abducted the daughters of the most noble families in
> Alemania and Italy without anyone resisting him, and he gave
> them in marriage to his relatives. Yea, in his folly [!], or rather in
> his madness, he went so far as to forcefully enter a convent with a
> number of his friends to abduct the daughter of Count Unruoch,
> a relative of the emperor, and give her in marriage to his cousin.
> But the nuns in the convent turned to the Lord for revenge of
> the defamation inflicted on their holy place. Their prayer was
> immediately answered. For the one who wanted to spend his
> wedding night in the usual way with the girl died that same night
> and the girl remained untouched. This was revealed to a nun of this
> convent who related it to the others.

In the light of the later Grail stories as related by Wolfram von Eschenbach, these events can be interpreted in a different way. Viewed from Wolfram's Parsifal, the practice of giving the daughters of noble families in marriage to Liutward's relatives should be seen in relation to the task of the Grail family to connect spiritual Grail Christianity with the growth and becoming of Europe. Of course this had to evoke a storm of political indignation and hatred on the part of other families and power centers.

A false accusation was to bring Liutward down. In a different chronicle we read what occurred to him in the same year 887 and what he had to go through. (Walter Johannes Stein saw in this event a parallel with the story of Parsifal and the hard fate Jeshute had to undergo. Stein incorporated the Richardis legend in his book *The Ninth Century*.) Here is the historical source, the *Regionis Chronica*[59] (*Chronicle of the Region*):

> 887. First of all the emperor removed Liutward of Vercelli
> scornfully from his following. The emperor loved Liutward. He was
> his only counselor and looked after all public affairs. But now the
> emperor accused him of adultery because he had meddled in an
> inappropriately confidential way in the secrets of the empress.

What now follows is clearly an insinuation of adultery although it is much less clearly related in the chronicle than in the legend, where Liutward is accused by a red knight of touching the empress inappropriately. The chronicle again:

> Then the emperor calls his consort Richardis, the empress, before
> the assembly because of the same affair and—it sounds incredible—
> the empress confesses that he has never united himself in loving
> embrace with her, although they have lived in legally concluded
> community of marriage for over ten years. She also declares that
> she has been free of physical intercourse not only with him but also
> with any other man. She takes pride in her untouched virginity
> and, if her spouse so desires, she wants to prove this through the
> judgment of almighty God in a battle of man against man or
> through the red-hot plowshares. For she was a woman who had
> dedicated herself to God.

Apparently both Richardis and Liutward were reinstated in full honor. The chronicle has no further details about that. But the legend has an extensive story about the further adventures of Richardis. The chronicle concludes succinctly: "After the divorce she withdrew into a convent [Andlau] she had founded out of her possessions, to serve God."

In this way Liutward, and also Richardis, went through a great trial in the year 887. Again, just as after the events with the Norsemen five years earlier, he continued his work after the false accusations and trials. In the chronicles he disappears from the scene. Only in the year 901 is he mentioned once more (in the *Regionis Chronica*) but now because of the circumstances of his death.

> In the year of the Divine Incarnation 901, the Hungarians invaded Lombardy and cruelly destroyed everything by murder, arson and plunder. When the inhabitants pulled together and dared to resist the invaders' cruelty and rage, many of them lost their lives due to arrow shots. Most of the bishops and counts perished. One day, when Liutward, bishop of Vercelli and the most trusted friend and secret counselor of Charles III (the Fat), from the bottom of his heart [!] tried to save his fortune and incomparable treasures, the abundance of which exceeded all measure, from the bloodthirsty rage of the Hungarians, he still unexpectedly ran into them and was quickly killed. The riches he had wanted to save were seized.

Thus Liutward came to a violent end.

From this report in the chronicle we may have a suspicion as to where Liutward was between the years 887 and 900, since it indicates that he was in Central Europe. True, it names Lombardy (Vercelli) but we can also find him in Carinthia on the border of today's Hungary. To become clear on this we must open the same chronicle again on the page where the description of the events of 887 continues. We follow the further, now tragic, fate of Charles the Fat in the *Regionis Chronica* (Walter Johannes Stein sees in his vicissitudes the source of the description of Orilus as given by Wolfram von Eschenbach in his *Parsifal*).

> After these events [the divorce of Richardis] the emperor became ill in body and soul. In November, around the death day of St. Martin [November 11], he came to Trier and called a Reichstag[60] together.

When the great leaders of the realm observed that the emperor was not only losing his physical strength but also his mental capacities, they took it on themselves to place Arnulf, son of Carloman, at the head of the government. In a sudden conspiracy all the noblemen renounced Charles and went over to Arnulf.

Charles is then left to his fate. After three days there is hardly anyone left who conveyed to him even the most elementary duties of human love. Food and drink are given to him at Liutward's expense. These events made a deep impression on people, and in relation to human destiny and sudden changes in circumstances they were astonishing. Whereas he had had the great realm in his hands without pains or effort, so that he had come close to the dignity and power of the Frankish kings, now Charles had lost everything in a tragic destiny. It was like a demonstration of the vulnerability of man, by destroying in one humiliating instant everything that had been accumulated in a time of happy success.

The emperor was turned into a beggar. He sent Arnulf a request for provisions. In his desperate circumstances he thought first of all of his essential needs. He sent his son Bernard, begotten with a concubine, to Arnulf with gifts to pay tribute to him. It was pitiful to see how the once immeasurably rich emperor was not only robbed of his happiness but also had to rely on charity. King Arnulf gave him a few estates in Allemania from the proceeds of which he could live. Arnulf himself returned to Bavaria after he had solved the problem with the Franks.

About Liutward we hear nothing any more. Where did he go? Did he accompany Arnulf to Bavaria? At any rate, he was reinstated; we saw that in the year 900 he still possessed dignity and great wealth. As was mentioned already, we have to look for him not only in Vercelli in Lombardy but also in central Europe. He had another twenty-four years to live. The Annals of St. Gallen[61] relate that Notker was able to borrow Greek texts from him. Liutward's wealth certainly did not consist only of gold, silver and land; more especially we should think of books, such as manuscripts illustrated with precious miniatures. In his time most manuscripts were 'insular,' meaning they were made by Irish and Anglo-Saxon monks. We should think of manuscripts representing a broader vision of Christianity than the dogmas prescribed by Rome. We may conclude this about Liutward's wealth from the *Annales Fuldenses*:

> When the aforementioned Liutward had continued his practices
> [of giving daughters of the nobility in marriage to his own relatives]
> for a few years, he made efforts, inflated by delusions of vanity and
> greed [!], to change the Catholic faith and belittle our Redeemer.
> He asserted that the Redeemer was one in substance but not in
> person, but the Catholic Church believes and confesses that He is
> two substances and one person. And whoever denies that mocks
> Him and does not seek Him Who came to redeem all that was
> lost. If there were not one true God, He would not be able to bring
> salvation. And if He had not truly become a human being, He
> would not have been our example.

> In the year 882 the anger of the emperor rose against this Liutward,
> this despiser. After consultation with his advisors in the churches
> he dismissed him so he was no longer arch-chaplain. He took away
> Liutward's feudal estates and expelled him from the palace as a
> hated heretic. But Liutward went to Arnulf in Bavaria and devised
> plans to rob the emperor of his power.

(We should note that we have a description here of a crisis in 882 and not, like other sources, in 887.) From the text we see that Liutward had a different view of Christ as God and Man. What we see here is the question of whether in his incarnation Christ became fully human. This was a constant question in the heretical streams within Christianity that were based on Manichaeism.

From the chronicle we can conclude that Liutward made a distinction between the man Jesus and the God Christ. After the baptism in the Jordan these were one in substance but not in person. Christ united with the human corporeality in Jesus. He became the second Adam. In Jesus the substance of the first Adam was still living in its condition before the fall. With this pure substance Christ was able to unite for three years. In Jesus He went through suffering, death and resurrection. Thus Christ and Jesus were one in substance but not in person.

In his Grail story Wolfram von Eschenbach speaks of the Grail as a being, the substance Jesus carries within himself. Wolfram relates how during Lucifer's fall from heaven Michael struck a stone from his crown. It is a picture of one single human being who, down into his physical substance, preserved his condition from before the fall, the paradisal condition of humanity. This human being formed the chalice, the physical and soul sheath into which Christ could descend. The substance which came for the first time to earth in Jesus formed the chalice into which, with the power of the Holy Spirit, Christ descended. Wolfram described the mystery that the Grail knights observed in the same way.

From this point of view also, Liutward had a connection with the Grail mysteries. The author of the Annals mockingly called him 'king of kings.' Liutward was no king of a physical realm, but he preserved the Grail secrets. As such he was a king of kings, because his kingship was 'not of this world.' Wolfram von Eschenbach relates in his epic how Parsifal, who lived eleven generations before him, after a laborious course full of error, straying and ridicule, was proclaimed King of the Grail. This event took place in the year 869.

It is noteworthy that the writer who called Liutward 'king of kings' did so from the monastery of Fulda, the original monastery of St. Boniface, and in doing so represented the official policy of the church. This may give us food for thought, especially since the chronicles again and again reflect efforts to ridicule Liutward, while these efforts seem to be completely baseless. It is possible that Liutward was proclaimed King of the Grail at the time of the Council of Constantinople in 869, as described by Wolfram von Eschenbach.[62] Liutward carried the inner grade of development of a Parsifal. As such he carried a great responsibility relative to the development of spiritual Christianity, which is expressed in the image of the Grail.

Historically the concept of Jesus Christ as God and Man, which lives in Grail Christianity, can be found in the works of the Irish-oriented thinkers of the 9th century. Their thinking is based on the letters of St. Paul and the work of the Irishman Pelagius (ca. 354–418). A contemporary of Liutward, Sedulius Scotus wrote commentaries on the letters of St. Paul in Liège (now in Belgium). In his book about the history of the Irish church, Walter Delius sees the lost commentaries by Pelagius on the letters of St. Paul as source of those of Sedulius Scotus.[63] Jacob Streit says about Pelagius in his book *Sun and Cross*:

In his dispute with Arianism, Pelagius asserts that they misunderstood the 'true divinity' of Christ. Opposing the Manichees he asserts that they misunderstand the 'true human nature' of Christ.[64]

Liutward shows the same view of the man Jesus and the Son of God, who was called the 'Logos' in the beginning of the Gospel of St. John. When Liutward was killed in 900 or 901 he was carrying a treasure trove of books with him. The lost commentaries by Pelagius on the letters of St. Paul may have been among these. Liutward died a martyr's death, but all his life he was uncompromising under ridicule, false attacks and accusations. He went through the valley as a Parsifal, but with the resurrection power of Christ!

We conclude this chapter with a quotation from *The Ninth Century* by Walter Johannes Stein:

> Throughout an entire epoch the history of his time was really guided by Liutward, and his spiritual influence was extraordinarily great. He died on St. John's Day, June 24, 900, in a battle against the Hungarians in Italy. Is the connection between Liutward and Arnulf of Carinthia[65] to be ascribed to mere chance, in view of the fact that Parsifal carries the arms of Styria[66]—the panther—that he inherited from his father?

Sedulius Scotus described the symbolism of the panther as follows:

> It does not become a just ruler to go about with friends who are tyrants, who are just like dangerous snakes, as the panther shows. For the panther belongs to the quadrupeds and, as nature investigators will say, the panther is friend to all animals except the snake. Thus, let all rulers reserve their friendships for those of whom they know that they are virtuous.[67]

In the traits of Liutward's being, which we here conclude in the image of the panther, we may perhaps recognize many aspects of the pupils who now seek our schools—and find them!

16

PARSIFAL AND THE TASK OF THE WALDORF SCHOOL MOVEMENT – 3

*N*ow that I have described the historical Parsifal in the previous chapter, I want to consider the challenge Parsifal poses for Waldorf education in our time. In chapter 14 I quoted Rudolf Steiner's words that Parsifal will incarnate early in the 21st century, in our time therefore, to help develop a new spiritual and world culture. The condition for this is that the Waldorf pedagogical impulse is flourishing. Viewed from the outside this is certainly the case. In Holland every child lives within easy reach of a Waldorf school. But what did Steiner mean with these words? Do they perhaps have something to do with the Grail mystery itself, whether the Waldorf school is able to preserve its true being and task, and develop these further?

In 1913 Steiner gave a lecture cycle in The Hague, Holland, published in English under the title *The Effects of Esoteric Development* (GA 145). In this cycle he described the search of Parsifal for the Grail and also the Grail mystery itself. The way traveled by Parsifal is a way in the night. When he meets the Fisher King on the lake, who shows him the way to the Grail Castle, he enters the world of sleep. Then follows a difficult path along the rock-face, until he suddenly stands on the edge of a precipice. In the light of the setting sun, on the border between waking and sleeping, he can just make out the golden cupolas of the Grail Castle.

What is really happening here? In sleep the human being experiences the skull as a rock-face along which he can enter the inside of his head as a way across the abyss, when he experiences the inside of the head, and its center as a holy place. This center is situated right in the middle of the brain, at the location of the pineal gland. In this area of the brain a process takes place that can be understood in the light of the image of the 'nourishment of the Grail.'

After he has crossed the abyss, Parsifal is conducted into the Grail Castle, and in the heart of the castle he enters a hall where a sick king receives nourishment from the Grail. Parsifal wonders about this. But because in his school years he learned not to ask too many questions, he is silent during his observation of this wondrous process of nourishment from a chalice cut from a precious stone, which seems to have an inexhaustible power of nourishment. Because during his apprenticeship with Gurnemanz Parsifal lost the habit of asking questions, it will take a very long time before he can build a conscious connection with this enigmatic process in the center of the Grail Castle, therefore also in the center of the brain.

The school years play a decisive role here. That was true in the 9th century, the time of the historical Parsifal (Liutward) as archetypal image, but it is especially true today at the beginning of the 21st century. This mysterious process in the center of the brain is one that can greatly occupy a teacher. Why did Gurnemanz discourage Parsifal from asking questions?

The block method of teaching in Waldorf schools gives great opportunity to investigate a subject as a group, teacher and students together. The teacher and the students can reach judgments and concepts out of pictures and experiences they have gone through together. As soon as we start with definitions before there have been experiences we kill the power of questioning. Closed opinions and judgments work in the same way. For instance, we can speak about peoples, individuals and animals, but also about cultures, history or art in an artistic manner that leaves room for one's own questions and insights. In this way one does not follow a path that leads to a judgment or concept that was predetermined by others.

As a child, Parsifal loves life; he is spontaneous, he lives with nature, the sun and the birds. He asks the knights he meets in the forest, and who make a deep impression on him, whether they are God. He asks his mother who God is. His mother does not give him a general answer but one with a wonderful characteristic; she says: "My son, He is light beyond all light, brighter than summer's day. ..." Her answer is as the morning verse in the Waldorf school. In grades one through four the children speak daily: "The sun with loving light makes bright for me each day."

It is Parsifal language that is spoken there. When expressing a characteristic like that we experience a force that does not fix things but awakens us to go on a search and ask more questions. Working with the subject in an artistic way, as we do while teaching a block, strengthens experience and evokes new questions.

Through the gates of the senses the children, and also their teachers, breathe in impressions that gain in strength when the soul is allowed to live in images and characterizations reinforced through artistic experiences such as painting, music, modeling, form drawing and eurythmy. During eurythmy, for instance, some wise guy exclaims: "What is this stuff good for?" Great question! "Have you noticed the kind of teamwork that grows among people during a eurythmy lesson? Isn't learning to work together exactly what goes on in eurythmy?" Such could be a constructive answer by the teacher.

A questioning attitude toward life strengthens sense observation—we can all experience that on a daily basis. When children want to know something or are interested in something, they are totally with it. They breathe in the impressions with all their senses. Through ears, eyes, touch, movement, smell and taste, everything is taken in, remains alive during the day as a delicate after-sound, and moves into the night with sleep.

The day is coming to an end, and again Parsifal goes along the rock-face approaching the Grail Castle. He brings with him the experiences of the day. Through bitter experience he has learned that he must ask questions! It is on the basis of this questioning soul mood that he now brings the experiences of the day into the night. He has learned to sleep in the right way. We also wish that for our students. Steiner pointed out in his very first lecture for Waldorf teachers that the principal goal of modern education must be to teach the child to sleep well.

At first hearing, it seems like a rather strange task for a teacher to teach the child to sleep well. But the task becomes more understandable when viewed in the light of the search for the Grail Castle. The Grail Castle is connected with the world we enter at night. And the extent to which we bring nourishing and healing forces back into the day when we awake depends on the way we enter this castle at night.

What happens in the night with the learning experiences taken in during the day? Every night a wondrous alchemical process takes place in the head, in which the after-effects of the sense impressions that live in the head in picture form connect themselves with the purest elements from our nutrition. These purest elements rise as a luminous life force into the head and gleam around the pineal gland.

As an image Parsifal becomes able to experience this in the shine of the Grail Chalice carried by the maiden. The maiden carries the purest elements from the metabolism up into the head. Pure power of will is connected with power of cognition in the head. That is the moment when Parsifal could ask the question as to the picture he is observing. The forces he brings with him as pure sense impressions from the world of the day can connect themselves with the Grail being itself. This Grail being is described as a being that again and again goes through a process of death and resurrection. Wolfram von Eschenbach lets Trevrezent, the hermit and brother of the sick Grail King, relate that the being of the Grail is the Phoenix, which is again and again rejuvenated in the flames.

On May 16, 1920,[68] Steiner returned to the subject of the secret of the Grail that takes place in the center of the human head. It is warmth that makes it possible that the picture character of the images taken in by the senses passes away and is transformed into a new substance, new insights in picture form. Warmth is in the human being the carrier of the I. The I lives in our head the moment we are stimulated to process images in our own way in sense-free experience and thinking. In the block method of teaching we do this often by reviewing the learning experiences of the previous day.

The warmth, which is needed for this process of breaking down and building up, can only remain alive and active in the head in one way. The student's own activity in perceiving and thinking born from the warmth of the engagement of the I, provides this warmth in the head with the possibility to transform, during sleep at night, the picture substance of the learning experience.

But Steiner went a step further, and now we approach the real mystery of the Grail:

> Precisely in the domain of heat a change is taking place in man
> which results in matter being destroyed and a purely picture-
> existence arising out of the matter; but through the union of
> the human soul with the Christ substance, this picture-existence
> becomes a new reality.[69]

In other words, through the warmth that can live in the head and can break down the pictures from the previous day, a transubstantiation takes place in which Christ gives the old pictures a new quality. Thus we can find in the human being what for centuries has been said by tradition, but only little understood, namely that the Grail Chalice was once used by Christ as the cup of the last Supper.

Originally, the same tradition said that the Grail was a magnificent stone in the crown of Lucifer. Lucifer, the Light Bearer, let the human being eat from the Tree of Knowledge of Good and Evil in paradise. Thereupon the human being was expelled from paradise and became conscious of himself. By the expulsion from paradise the human being was thrust into the outer world through the gates of the senses. His eyes were opened. The human being became a spectator, an outsider; in his eyes the world became unchangeable, and his path of learning ended in teaching by illustration. Human learning became a learning of fixed images to which the teacher had the task of adding the corresponding concepts. That was the goal of Amos Comenius in the method of education by illustration which he developed.

In the 1970s the call for creative education became stronger and stronger. And yet, since that time the goals of education have become tighter and tighter. Large amounts of money are invested to develop effective teaching methods. But does this not create the danger for us in education land of laying fixed tracks along which we expect answers from the children which we put there ourselves?

Pure thinking, also called sense-free thinking, wants to connect in its own activity the purest elements from perception with the substances of the metabolism, the seat of the will life. This means that the child has to be given the freedom to connect himself with the lesson content in his own way, and especially to process this content after the learning experiences have gone 'through the night.'

The lesson book can be an expression of this process. When we review a lesson book as teacher or parent, we immediately experience whether it radiates warmth and light. Of course there are the colors, but there is also its entire form, and its originality. The lesson book can be an expression of a process of transubstantiation, of the child's own 'digestion' of the lesson content. As teacher you can then really be moved by the work of the pupils. The lesson content has become an almost living substance of color and content. In the 9th century, the time of the first Grail knights, people called the 'Book of the Grail' a 'living book.' A lesson book can evoke a similar experience.

Christ spoke the words: "Where two or three are gathered in my name, I shall be in the midst of them." Also in the head, our Grail Castle, two or more streams come together in the night. When the child falls asleep, he will process the images of all he has experienced that day. He carries this into the sanctuary of the head, also the experiences from school. These came in through the twelve gates of the senses, and when they have really been lived through, they are filled with warmth. Through warmth, the lesson contents have a connection with the child's own will life that rises up out of the metabolism as most pure activity. In their midst the Christ Sun can work in warmth and light.

As a child Parsifal was called 'pure fool.' His mother always called him 'dear boy.' He learned all the time through experience and not through laws and rules. He developed his concepts while going right through the middle of life. His name, Parsifal, means: 'straight through the middle' or 'right through the valley.'

It benefits children of the 21st century if their learning is one of experience, and the block method (but also all the other subjects) can facilitate or hinder this. Concepts may be acquired by the child himself, and pictures may be generated by his own imagination. In the night they can then, in a Grail process of warmth and light, turn into a new substance, nourishment, Grail food. What was learned the previous day is then on its way to becoming new life forces. The observation of this transubstantiation is like a sun force for the teacher. Then there is a secret that weaves between teacher and pupil in which the Grail is invisibly present, and each feels himself to be a Parsifal who goes 'through the middle of the valley.'

In the night everything is made new. Christ spoke the words: "Behold, I make all things new." This entire process is an I-activity that occurs during the night but has immense consequences for daily life. The power of the Grail rejuvenates and heals the old pictures that have been experienced in daily life in school by trial and error. We live in an exciting time, and constantly run the risk of incurring injury through intense impressions that may be difficult to process.

We see this also in the Grail story. In the Grail Castle Parsifal sees not only the Grail but also a bleeding Spear. It is the same spear with which the Roman officer Longinus pierced Christ's side on Good Friday. Parsifal sees the bleeding Spear before he sees the Grail. In this image he experiences the wounds incurred by the soul by impressions from the sense world which desire, anger or hatred have called forth in him. It is the injury of passion that appears here. The power of passion kills the healing power of the Grail. Passion, anger and hatred rise up whenever I-activity is not engaged.

The I of the children, of the pupils entrusted to us teachers, still surrounds them, and it is of the greatest importance that we serve these becoming individualities and not harass them with our concepts, but rather that we share our experiences with them. In this sense, as teachers we can become followers of the second teacher of Parsifal. His first teacher, Gurnemanz, taught him rules and customs and discouraged him from asking questions. Trevrezent, however, spoke to him not only as a teacher but also as his equal. This enabled Parsifal to gradually find his own identity and to enter the Grail Castle for a second time, but now consciously, to help influence the future of the earth with healing ideas that can be viable and renewing for future generations.

When Parsifal now grows up on earth, he can fully develop his capacities only through this approach by his teachers. And Parsifal does not come just by himself; he has many partners in destiny who long ago were Grail- and Arthur knights, just as he was, and now want to work for a better world.

Walter Johannes Stein was fully aware of these connections when he wrote his book about Parsifal and his time, *The Ninth Century*, which we have frequently quoted. He lived intensively with this processing of lesson contents and experiences at night. He had an intensive meditative life. He developed the strength for meditation out of an enormous will power. This will power also caused him to make many mistakes in his relationships with other people. He was often too quick or too direct, and that made him enemies. But Steiner was able to enjoy him, even if he sometimes rolled his eyes at his excessive impulsivity.

But because he also brought his willpower into his inner life, Stein was able to imbue his thinking and the way he processed the content of perceptions with enormous warmth. This power brought him to the conviction that he would be able to experience the Grail mystery consciously. Steiner confirmed this and then gave him a meditation that ended with the words: "Rely on the light-warm I." In the course of the year that followed, Stein developed a meditative life that was totally integrated with an enormously active life as a Waldorf teacher, in such a way that he was able to find himself in the 9th century in the vicinity of Parsifal. This was the inner impetus for his book.

For me the book formed the starting point for collecting further material on the historical Parsifal. Stein's book was much appreciated but also ridiculed as unscientific (although he had taken his doctor's degree on the working of the senses and had been accompanied and valued in this by Steiner). The book grew out of the blocks on Parsifal he had given to eleventh graders, and had lived through and investigated together with them, for seven years. It is like pictures that went through the night, like a very big lesson book and as such repeatedly added to by other people. He wrote the book with the intention of developing it further in the beginning of the 21st century together with new pupils and new teachers.[70]

17

RUDOLF HAUSCHKA AND WALA

*N*utrition is a problem Rudolf Steiner often mentioned in relation to Waldorf school pedagogy. Rudolf Hauschka (1891–1969) was a pioneer in this field. He became known because of his initiative to found a company that produces anthroposophical remedies without using alcohol. He also wrote a number of pioneering books about nutrition, medicine and substances. His book *Nutrition* is widely read.

Rudolf Hauschka

In the 1970s this book was for me personally a door through which I was able to experience anthroposophy as true. At that time I had started a biodynamic farm together with some friends. During quiet moments, sitting in the open door of the hay loft and looking out over the land directly behind the dike along the river Waal, I used to read Hauschka's words about milk and bread. He wrote not just about nutritional substances but also about their cosmic origin, which gives his books a dimension that reminds us of the nourishment that is described as that proceeding from the Grail.

Who was Rudolf Hauschka? He was born in 1891 on the death day of the great Irish-Celtic pioneer Columbanus who, with his companions from Iona, brought a free Christianity to the continent of Europe. At the end of his life Columbanus died in the monastery he had founded in Bobbio, Italy. Rudolf Hauschka was born in Vienna where he spent the years of his youth. His grandfather and father had a metalworking business. After high school, where he immersed himself in geometry and chemistry, he studied chemistry at the university and wrote a thesis on natural and chemical dyes.

Before World War I he had already heard of anthroposophy from Karl Schubert, his classmate, who spoke, in a student organization that opposed alcohol

106

and called itself the 'Templars,' about anthroposophy and Steiner. Schubert's classmates jokingly called him 'a spiritual high and mighty one.' Karl Schubert would in 1920 begin the first parallel class in the Waldorf school. At that time Rudolf Hauschka was to meet him again, but that was later. For now he could not yet really find a direct connection with anthroposophy.

During World War I Hauschka had a second 'indirect' encounter with anthroposophy. In his autobiography[71] he described it as follows:

> Suddenly something happened I had not foreseen. Whether it was caused by my three years' duty at the front, by my deficient hearing, or by my quality as a chemist—in any case I was transferred to the munitions factory in Blumau. So I left the front, visited first my family in Vienna, and after a few days reported to the munitions factory. There I was told, with apologies, that my place had already been filled. Thus I went home without regret to wait for the things that were to come.

> After some time I received the order to report to the Ministry of Defense [in Vienna] as adjutant to the Minister of War. I had to give a lecture on carbide and nitrogen and later had a personal interview. I then received the administration of secret documents and had to give those to the minister for his signature.

> One day I was addressed in the hallway by an artillery officer who had just returned from the front. Deep in Russia he had received a telegram that he was urgently needed. He had received leave, but the trip abroad [to Berlin] that was needed could be approved only by the minister himself. He had been trying for several days to get access to the minister, but everyone thought he was crazy to think he would be allowed to make a trip to Berlin in the middle of the war. He had been sent away everywhere he had tried. I was his last hope, and he implored me to help him.

> The man made the impression on me of carrying a decision out of an unyielding will. Outwardly calm and collected, with an almost elegant stature, a will power streamed out of him which I experienced almost physically. It was a noble will power; that is

how I felt it. I did not ask him what he was going to do in Berlin—
although I would have liked to know it—but took his request for
leave and told him to wait. Because I was just going to the minister
with a file full of documents for his signature, I slipped the man's
request in between them. My minister signed everything without
questions or comments, including the request.

Ten years later I ran into this same officer, now in civvies, during
an anthroposophical world conference in London. It was Walter
Johannes Stein, the well-known Waldorf school teacher and author
of the famous book about the Grail. At the time he had received
a telegram from Rudolf Steiner to come to Berlin. Destiny had
picked me out to help him.

Rudolf Hauschka met Steiner during a conference in Arnhem in 1924. He
had several conversations with him and then asked him what would be the best
way to investigate life forces. Steiner directed his attention to the importance of
rhythms to get insight into life processes. From that moment Rudolf Hauschka
found his own research subject within anthroposophy. But still, he would always
go his own way. For instance, he made voyages all over the world in his large
sailing ship, the *Istar*.

He felt a connection with Ita Wegman, and in 1935 this resulted in the
founding of his own factory of medical remedies with the meaningful name of
WALA. This company still exists beside the company called Weleda. Both names
were known in Charlemagne's time, especially among the Saxons. They point to the
priestesses who prepared remedies and gave advice to the people and preserved the
ancient sagas and legends. Berta, Charlemagne's mother, and Alcuin, the leader of
the Court School, stimulated Charlemagne to get these traditions written down,
despite their non-Christian character.

Rudolf Hauschka saw the connection with Berta especially in the place where
the WALA factory was located, Eckwälden:

Eckwälden, part of Boll, is situated at the foot of the Turmberg
on the flat top of which there must have been an old cultic place
of the Celts. On the other side of Boll stands Bertha Castle where
traces of old cultic places have been found. The name Bertha, in

old times Berchta or Perchta, indicates the worship of an ancient
Celtic goddess that can be related to the Greek Persephone. In
the 7th century a real countess Bertha resided here. She had the
castle demolished and the stones used to build the church of Boll.
And now it was discovered during renovation work that under the
church in Boll there is an Irish-Scottish [Irish-Celtic] crypt.[72]

With the founding of the WALA factory, Rudolf Hauschka was transported
back into Carolingian times, for Berta was also the name of Charlemagne's mother.
But we can also be led back into Carolingian times in quite a different way, for the
name Wala occurs at the court of Charlemagne. Wala was a count with a Saxon
mother and Frankish father, whose wedding probably took place in 772 after the
destruction of the Irminsul at the Externsteine near Paderborn, Germany.[73] In
773 Wala was born as the eldest child. He became a pupil of Alcuin, the leader
of the Court School. Until Charlemagne's death he worked and fought for the
empire. After 814 he entered a monastery at age 41 and gave the impetus toward
the building of a monastery in the vicinity of the Externsteine. Ultimately the
monastery was moved to Corvey on the Weser.[74]

Corvey became the place where the Germanic/Saxon folk spirit connected
itself with Christianity. In its monastery the famous History of the Saxons was
written by Widukind of Corvey in the 10th century.[75]

We also find Wala in Walter Johannes Stein's book about the Grail, *The
Ninth Century*. Here he is described as a companion of Count Hugo of Tours.
Stein describes how after Charlemagne's death a number of faithful friends who
had been connected with Irish-Celtic Grail Christianity were discredited with
Louis the Pious and were ultimately sent into exile in Italy, together with Louis'
rebellious son Lothar.

> Hugo experienced a strange destiny. He went to Italy,
> accompanying Lothar, together with the other nobles, on whom
> rested the valour, the strength and the wisdom of the country. Here
> Lothar distributed gifts. Matfried received the Veltlin possessions
> of St. Denis [the monastery in which Waldo had once been
> abbot]. Hugo's daughter received St. Salvatore in Brescia, Hugo's
> wife an estate in Lambro. But almost all who had emigrated with
> Lothar died simultaneously in 837 during a fever epidemic: Wala,

Matfried, Hugo, Lambert, Godfrey and his son Agimbert, Burgarit, Jesse and Bishop Elias. One only was saved: Richard. The almost simultaneous death of all those who represented the bloom of the Frankish nobility, but who had abandoned their liege and ruler, could not fail to produce a strong impression. Louis the Pious was deeply stirred by the news. Beating his breast, with eyes filled with tears, he implored God to grant peace to their souls.[76]

These friends died in different locations. According to his biographer, Wala died in 836 in the Irish-Celtic oriented monastery of Columbanus in Bobbio, where he had become the abbot upon his arrival.

Rudolf Hauschka was born on the death day of Columbanus and gave his initiative the name of WALA, with four capitals. Each of these letters meant something to him and was an expression of a specific medicinal preparation out of the healing impulse of anthroposophy, which he would develop starting in 1929.

In his autobiography he speaks a couple of times of Walter Johannes Stein. As we have already seen, in London the renewed acquaintance made an impression that connected Rudolf Hauschka with the impulse of anthroposophy. That which had one day been prepared in the pre-war meeting with Karl Schubert now brought forth fruit through the renewed acquaintance with Walter Johannes Stein in England. But a few years later this Waldorf school teacher would settle permanently in England, at the invitation of Daniel Nicol Dunlop, the organizer of the anthroposophical world conference in London of 1928. The rise of National Socialism forced Stein to go there because he was half Jewish, as did the problems in the Waldorf school and in the Anthroposophical Society in Stuttgart.

But as is related in the following note in his biography, Rudolf Hauschka did not forget his encounter with Stein. The two friends, with a shared destiny from Carolingian times, found each other again and awakened an earnestness in each other to work for a spiritual pedagogy and art of medicine. Hauschka said:

My 'Istar' was moored in the port of London during the time that in that city the anthroposophical world conference was being held. I had, therefore, the opportunity to attend the conference and to greet my old friends, especially Dr. Ita Wegman, at whose initiative the conference had come about, and my friend from the Ministry of Defense, Walter Johannes Stein. The 'Istar' was a sensation at the conference, and I could hardly handle the stream of visitors. But I invited Dr. Ita Wegman and Walter Johannes Stein for dinner on the 'Istar.'… A remarkable feeling came over me as if adventures from a far distant past were connecting themselves with future ones.[77]

Wala died in Italy in exile, but his home country was in the north, in the Saxon area where Scandinavian and Celtic spirituality had roots. Rudolf Hauschka wrote about a trip he was offered around his first moon node at age 19. Steiner pointed out to him that events at this age of life have to do with impulses from former lives.

> After my graduation from high school I was offered a trip to Italy. I would rather have gone north, to Scandinavia, Scotland or Ireland. In Italy I felt myself a stranger. Only after I had the Karawanken tunnel behind me, and had reached the valley of Drau, was I happy again.[78]

Rudolf Hauschka tells of his earliest childhood memories. It is as if in these experiences the old gods of the north, especially the god of thunder and lightning Thor, spoke to him once more.

> My earliest memory in this life—I was then 2½ years old—enables me fully to say 'yes' to my destiny, even now. I was sitting on the floor in my parental home and was playing. Suddenly a bolt of lightning lit up the room followed by a mighty thunderclap. I must have been badly frightened, for my grandfather who was in the same room put his hand on my head and spoke: "The Father in Heaven speaks." These words consoled me and set me completely at rest.

> This unforgettable impression has carried me through many trials in my life. In later critical situations I would remember the words: "The Father in Heaven speaks"—and there was a lot of thunder! In this way the respect and trust in the guidance of destiny did not leave me even in an atheistic period of my life.[79]

At the time of Charlemagne, the Saxons wore in lieu of a cross the hammer of Thor around their necks. This made them feel accompanied by the power of the Heavenly Father in the battles and trials of life. Although Charlemagne had strictly forbidden this practice, Wala must still have seen it with his Saxon grandparents, and through his teacher Alcuin it must have been explained to him together with the collected stories about Thor and the other Germanic gods. The hammer of Thor was not only experienced in the force of lightning and thunder, but also in the individual courage of the heart.

In Walter Johannes Stein, Rudolf Hauschka encountered this same force when he ran into him as an officer in the hallway of the Ministry of Defense in Vienna. Stein discovered his inner connection with Hugo of Tours as he was writing his book about the Grail, which appeared at the world conference in London in 1928. In the book he described the life of Hugo of Tours in relation to Carolingian times. At that very same time the renewed acquaintance with an old companion took place. And in the year that followed, Rudolf Hauschka began the work from which the name WALA would be born:

> The Father of Truth guards the spring from which a few initiates
> are permitted to drink. However, he sends his child, Artistic
> Imagination, to the souls on earth who are thirsting for truth.
> Testing and trying I came to the first experiment. It was in May
> 1929, and the roses were blooming abundantly. Rose petals were
> collected in two beakers which were then filled with water. The first
> beaker remained untouched, standing on the laboratory table, while
> the other one was subjected to rhythmical processes. Rose bushes
> have very strong connection with the rising and the setting of the
> sun. The beaker with the rose petals was placed in the morning and
> evening sun ...[80]

Rudolf Hauschka then describes how the color of the water became deeper and deeper red, and that there was no growth of mold, while this did occur in the other beaker. The rose extract won in this way remained in good condition even after thirty years, despite the fact that it had to be uncorked frequently to show it to interested people. Following this experiment Hauschka continued with artistic imagination and arrived at several rhythmic treatments through light, warmth and even a burning, ash-forming process.

The resulting preparations received labels. W for preparations from warmth processes, L for those from light processes, WA for those for which the warmth process had been enhanced with ash, and LA for light processes enhanced with ash. Suddenly Hauschka saw in these letters the name WALA, which became the name of his company, although he did not know what it meant. Only later did he discover that WALA is the Germanic goddess who permeates nature and inspired her priests and priestesses toward healing work among the northern peoples.

We can find WALA's rose soap and other products in some Waldorf schools. Also the remedies that are prepared without alcohol can be a blessing for teachers, parents and students.

The name Rudolf Hauschka found was not only the right one for the company, which still exists, but it also indicated a trail that led him to his own being and his service of a spiritual impulse at the time of Charlemagne and his successors. And this connected him with the destiny of the Waldorf school movement, just as his path to anthroposophy was accompanied by two Waldorf school teachers, Karl Schubert and Walter Johannes Stein.

In conclusion, here is a little anecdote, for Rudolf Hauschka could have fun about Stein when the latter was living in a kind of exile in England.

> The collaboration with Dunlop and Stein was enormously fruitful for me. New horizons were opening—you could feel the breath of the wide world. Dunlop took the initiative for the summer conferences. …Several hundred participants gathered to work together. You felt like being teacher and student at the same time, and we mutually stimulated each other. During conversations and visits to the old cultic places of the Druids and old dwelling places of Irish-Scottish monks of the 5th century, I came to a strong experience of Irish-Celtic Christianity …

> Since there were many German-speaking lecturers at these conferences, language problems sometimes caused comical situations. Ita Wegman thought it was important that every collaborator at the summer conference bring a smoking jacket[81], so they could behave as 'lords' on festive occasions. Thus Walter Johannes Stein had brought his smoking and put it on for the festive opening of the conference. As he wanted to enter the hall, he

saw on the wall a sign 'Smoking not allowed.' He turned around, went back to his room, changed clothes and returned in his daily suit.[82]

Rudolf Hauschka remained a faithful friend of the Waldorf school teacher he had met for the first time in 1918 in their mutual striving for a spiritual art of medicine and education, and in their relationship humor was never lacking. It is as if the Heavenly Father of their common destiny smiles on us, and that gives us courage also for our work in Waldorf education, now in the 21st century.

18

WALTER JOHANNES STEIN AND HUGO OF TOURS

*I*t was in a certain sense an accident that Walter Johannes Stein became part of the college of teachers at the Waldorf school in Stuttgart. In 1922 Rudolf Steiner confirmed to him that the Parsifal epic of Wolfram von Eschenbach was

Walter Johannes Stein

an excellent topic for a block in 11th grade. Full of enthusiasm he went to work and he asked Steiner for advice whenever he had questions. In 1928 this work culminated in the publication of Stein's book *The Ninth Century*, which he intended as the first volume of a World History in the Light of the Grail.

In 1924 he went through a remarkable spiritual experience. He began to experience prior incarnations, which Steiner was still able to confirm to him. In the historical time of the Grail, the 9th century, he recognized himself as a knight at the court of Charlemagne, Hugo of Tours. Charlemagne sent this Hugo of Tours as his ambassador to Constantinople [Istanbul] in 811. He is also called Hugo the Timid.[83]

Walter Johannes Stein did research into the historical personalities behind the Grail story. Thus, among others, he came across Hugo of Tours, a knight and confidant of Charlemagne. Daan van Bemmelen spoke with Stein about his experiences around the Grail. He wrote the following in a letter to Werner Greub who had published a book about Wolfram von Eschenbach and the Grail:

> That which was not part of a lecture was told to me by Stein
> himself. He told me that Hugo of Tours and the hermit Trevrezent
> are one and the same person. After the conflict of Lothar I with his

father Louis the Pious, he withdrew, but for the outer world he died in 837. Stein told me that he had experienced himself as Trevrezent, and that Rudolf Steiner had confirmed this.[84]

On July 25, 1932, Walter Johannes Stein gave a lecture on Trevrezent.[85] Ita Wegman found that lecture extremely important for young people and printed it in its entirety in the periodical *Natura*. Stein began the lecture in a way from which the attentive listener can gather that its content arose out of authentic personal experiences:

Dear Friends,

In order to give you a concrete picture of what a person was able to experience in the Middle Ages, I will tell you of a knight who had an eventful life. After he had gone through many adventures and battles, he sought refuge in a mountainous area so as to live there as a hermit. His friends had always given this knight, whom I shall call 'the Old One,' the nickname 'Fastdeed.'[86] Indeed, in his youth the Old One had been fast in his deeds. But in his old age he had acquired quiet wisdom in his intimate life with nature.

We find him in a lonely spot, off the road taken by merchants who sometimes travel through this region. There is a forest and a small lake. He lives under overhanging rocks and doesn't need much …

One day a young man came to the Old One. He took a rest after traveling far. He asked the Old One many questions, which the Old One answered. And what I can bring back to my mind of these conversations, I will now try to relate to you faithfully.

The young man is the Arthurian knight Schionatulander. Walter Johannes Stein indicates here that he had seen this conversation himself and had lived through it again in a retrospective experience. The questions Schionatulander asked of Trevrezent were about education. In their time education consisted of the Seven Liberal Arts. Trevrezent enabled the young man to become aware of how this education can lead to a path of initiation, to a new form of learning.

From memoirs of students of Walter Johannes Stein at the Waldorf school, we know that his way of teaching created a continuous lively dialog between students and teacher, even if Stein did a lot of the talking. The students felt themselves transported in his pictures and in the way he brought world history and the Parsifal epic.

Who was this Hugo of Tours with whom Walter Johannes Stein knew himself to be connected? When he was working on his Grail book he sent an extensive manuscript to his friends in order to share the results of his research with them. Daan van Bemmelen also received such a manuscript; I found it in his estate.

> Now I have to tell you who this Hugo of Tours really is. His daughter was the wife of Lothar I, and Hugo has the title Count of Tours. His biographical details are in my book. Here however, I want to emphasize that we are referred to Tours in relation to the Grail story. Hugo receives a relic [of the blood of Christ] and because at night he hears the angels sing, and also because he feels unworthy, he asks God whether it is right for him to possess such a treasure. …The individuals who are described as receivers of Grail relics are involved in the East-West question. This is true for Charlemagne, for Hugo of Tours and for the students of Waldo von Reichenau. In the biographies of Hugo of Tours and Waldo von Reichenau we find confirmation of Rudolf Steiner's statement that the Grail events took place around the year 800.[87]

19

THE TEACHING OF TREVREZENT

THE SEVEN LIBERAL ARTS IN THE RELATIONSHIP BETWEEN TEACHER AND PUPIL

*T*he Seven Liberal Arts can form a sense organ to help us take a look at our own lesson preparation and also at the development of the students. As the active expression of the seven planetary forces and their relative archangels, they provide us with rich potential both for lesson- and learning inspiration for the student, and also for process evaluation of the teacher. A wonderful example of what is meant here was given by Walter Johannes Stein in a lecture he gave on July 25, 1932, in Glastonbury, England.[88] He sketches an archetypal image of the teacher-pupil situation in the encounter between the Grail teacher Trevrezent and Grail seeker Schionatulander. In their conversation the Seven Liberal Arts and their active forces can be intensively experienced by both teacher and pupil. Because the conversation sheds so much light on the Seven Liberal Arts, I have quoted below a large part of the lecture. Ita Wegman thought this lecture was of the greatest importance and wanted young people to become acquainted with it.

> One day, a youth came to the old man to take a rest on a long journey. The youth asked many questions to which the old man responded. The old man said: "Look, the grass grows and the flowers in the grass are blossoming. But you overlook many things if you stop there and seek no further explanation of what you see. If you want to understand reality, you have to learn to see through the appearances which provide such a spectacle for the eyes. Something makes the grass grow. To discover what it is, you have to pass from the observation of external appearances to interior listening. If you pay close attention, you will recognize that the act of remembering an observation is a listening process.

A wonderful musicality in things will one day be revealed to you if you live with this thought and repeatedly pass from observation to inner listening. The whole of the plant world will resound. The cup opening upward will be transformed into the sound of trumpets. All growth will then resound with music. And as you learn to listen to nature even more deeply, you will learn that the resonance of growth and development is an echo. The real music resounds in the cosmos. The sun and the stars resound; you hear the music of the planets and understand how they are calling the plants. Every opening blossom is a little sun. Every plant twining its way upward is a planetary revolution. Look at a tree: Its whole being resounds. The sound of the tonic rumbles muffled in the solid trunk. The interval of a second resounds when the tree first divides, where it first branches out. And so it goes on. But most plants finish with the interval of the fifth. If you want to find a sixth or seventh, you have to listen to the sounds which occur when the blossoms open delicately and the insects carry the pollen away to other plants. The new seed is the octave.

"The whole cosmos is music and I listen to it year after year without ever tiring of it. Nothing in the cosmos which is repeated is ever quite the same. So every year, every century has its own music."

"That is wonderful," the youth said. "Allow me to be your pupil and to learn from you."

"I cannot teach you anything," the old man replied. "Your soul is much richer than mine. But I can teach you who your teachers are."

"And who are my teachers?" the youth asked in surprise.

"The cosmos itself," the old man told him. "The only reason you met me was to recognize the poverty of the people of my century. You will enrich them. But look, a bluebell. Observe it closely. Do you see its blue mantle? Protectively it is wrapped around a small yellow light within. This flower is an image of the soul. It, too, carries the light of the spirit within. It must never be extinguished. A blue mantle surrounds this light to prevent it from being extinguished. You also wore such a mantle before your mother conceived you. Keep it in your consciousness."

The old man also had a good relationship with animals. No animal was afraid of him. They trusted him and did not run away when he approached. And if they were ill or wounded they came to him to be healed. The old man knew which herbs healed which injuries and he also knew the proper time to pick the herbs. The healing properties of one might be brought out by the waxing moon when the sap rises like the tide; another would gain its strength through its fiery, aromatic properties with a waning moon when the sap was held back like the tide at abb.

The young knight learned all this with the feeling that it was something he had known before. On one occasion he dreamed about the old man; he, the youth, was old and the old man was young. He saw himself as the teacher and the old man his pupil.

I want to interrupt here. How wonderful, how profound does Walter Johannes Stein speak here about the secret of the teacher-pupil relationship. How great is the support we can feel here in our being as teachers, but also in our being as parents. The elder leads the youth through the realms of nature and awakens latent capacities in him. The elder does this out of a desire to serve. But in what follows the youth, out of his own inner knowing, poses a question as to that which comes after 'learning to read in the book of nature'; now teacher and pupil enter the realm of the Seven Liberal Arts.

The more the youth experienced these things, the more of a riddle they became. One day he asked the old man, who seemed to be in a communicative mood: "Tell me, how do you know so much?"

"Nature has taught me," the old man said. "Its great textbook is inexhaustible."

"No," cried the youth, "you are hiding something. You also know the subjects taught in our Schools. You are more than a hermit, you have learnt more in the past."

The old man said: "Now I know that the hour of parting has come. I will tell you who your teachers are, because they were mine as well. But once you have heard it you will leave. And rightly so. You only met me to go on and discover other things. So listen:

"Dialectic is taught in the Schools. No one knows who taught this subject first. But I will tell you: It is none other than the moon. Observe it as it traverses the sky. It does not look at anything from one side only. It looks at everything from all sides. Do likewise. Do not think you know everything and can therefore rest. No, look alertly around you. Everything will look different tomorrow. Furthermore, learn from the moon. Observe how it has reduced its fullness since yesterday. It consumes itself as it revolves. Learn that lesson and you will understand when I say that the moon was my teacher. Happy the man who can subsume his own opinion in the art of dialectic and learn something better. Happy the man who makes his own light disappear, like the moon, in order to receive and reflect illumination from the more exalted sun. Let the moon teach you reflection. Then your knowledge will continue to wax after it has first waned. Are you not aware of the words of John who baptized Jesus? He said: 'He must increase while I must decrease.' He was a master of dialectic, as you can see from his words. He also gained his wisdom from the moon. The moon is a good teacher. None but Gabriel, who endows the moon with its soul, has ever taught dialectic."

The young knight sat in silence beside the old man. The moon slowly made its way through the branches of the giant trees in the forest. Thereupon the youth said to the old man: "So dialectic is selflessness?"

"Yes," said the old man, "that is it."

Then the old man spoke about the souls of those who have died, which become entirely selfless in the sphere of the moon and are thus an archetypal image for this art. Think of what inspiration we can draw from this picture as teachers and parents! Being a teacher does indeed mean being able to constantly change one's orientation, again and again to discover new points of view. The block method requires that we always have to make new subject matter our own and thus works as a strong stimulus for this process of constant renewal. In this way, being a teacher becomes a true art, in which the pupil has an awakening effect on the teacher.

Seven teachers does old Trevrezent describe to young Schionatulander. Earlier the old man spoke of the moon, of Gabriel as the great teacher of dialectic, the art of always continuing to learn, in always considering things from new points of view. In the lower school it is the teacher who goes this path in his lesson preparation in order to transform the subject into pictures, into block content which he then works through together with his students. And do we not all experience the active effectiveness of always to be looking for new points of view and openings into the same subject, for instance, in arithmetic the phenomenon of fractions? In the upper school, however, the teacher asks of the students to practice the art of dialectic themselves.

But the pupil has to get to know another six great teachers. The conversation between young Schionatulander and old Trevrezent continues:

> The youth then asked: "Now, old man, reveal your knowledge of the whole progression to me. What can be learnt from Mercury?"
>
> "Mercury is the sphere," the old man said, "in which the soul discards pictorial vision, separating itself from ordinary images. The only thing it can take into that sphere is non-pictorial thinking. If you want to live in this sphere, you can do so through numbers.
>
> If you say: one apple, one pear, the apple and the pear are images in your mind. But if you say one, two, three, you inhabit a non-pictorial world. Mercury or Hermes has always been the teacher of arithmetic to all the peoples. The Greeks called him the god of merchants because these have to deal with figures. We, however, call him Raphael, the angel of healing. The art of healing is a secret arithmetic. Physicians always deal with the number three. Know then that every number has its secret:
>
>> One is the first, undivided entity.
>> Two is the contrast of polarities.

Three is the harmony between the poles.
Four reveals what is hidden.
Five is the number of decision.
Six the number of love.
Seven determines the totality of time.
Eight is the number of justice.
Nine is the number of the divine order.
Ten is the number of the human being.

"The Saviour was the third between the two tempters. The one tempter always wants too much, the other too little. The golden mean lies between too much and too little. On the golden path, foolhardiness is too much, cowardice is too little, courage is the golden mean. There are four realms of nature: mineral, plant, animal and human. There are also four elements: fire, air, earth and water. The Quinta Essentia is hidden. It is the true nature of light. In the physical world you can see only illuminated matter. In thinking, light itself is revealed to you: enlightenment, the flash of inspiration. Five is the dividing line. I taught you that when we spoke about the plant. A tree propagates, or not, when the seed falls on the stony ground. Events can go in either direction.

"The number six belongs to the bees. They use it to build their combs. Here love is impersonal, devoted completely to the service of the whole. Seven is seen in the rainbow, the week. Eight is twice four: divine and earthly justice. Nine is the divine choirs and ten represents human beings, for they are the tenth hierarchy."

Then old Trevrezent spoke about being a physician, and how the physician works with the number three, and how healing is hidden in this number. Think of the healing effect of arithmetic when we approach it out of movement, the way we do in Waldorf education. It works in a healing way on the often too heavy or too light limbs of the children. A block of arithmetic brings health, movement and a cheerful lightness into the class. A good teacher can be mercurial. And doesn't the first grader get a good understanding of the qualities of the numbers one to ten, the way Trevrezent taught them to Schionatulander? We continue with Schionatulander's question about Venus:

"And what does Venus teach us?" the youth asked.

The old man became sad when the youth asked this and said:
"Hardly anyone has any notion of Venus. Only people who purify
their will, who no longer carry any desire into this sphere, have
proper access to it. All selfish thirst for action has to be extinguished
here. One who succeeds in that recognizes what real will is: music,
nothing but music. The musical element is the essence of objectified
will. That is why Eros must be left behind if one would see the Lady
Venus naked and experience the most beautiful music in existence.
No one has ever learnt music except from Venus. She changes the
voice of human beings as they mature on earth. Anyone whose song
is noble and pure also has to be selfless and loyal. Treachery and
betrayal do not go with the noble art of singing."

The art of music, the art Venus bestows on us, has a great purifying effect.
Think of the joy it gives the students in the higher grades to sing in parts, and of
the satisfaction when everyone, even the shy ones, have mustered the courage to
sing with the rest. And for the teacher it is so good to experience that the song
sounds differently every day. Now, the old man starts speaking about the sun:

"The sun shines on things visible while light itself remains behind
the world of the senses. Michael, the Sun Prince, remains hidden
behind physical phenomena as does light, but without him world
evolution would have no meaning. Understand the meaning which
rests hidden behind what is as clear as the sun and you will have
learnt the cosmic script of Michael and will become a student in
the art of grammar. First you must learn to discover the letters.
Every butterfly wing, the wing of every tiny ladybug will show you
the letters of the cosmic script. All the mysterious symbols which
are engraved on crystals and stones are this script. There is no
butterfly wing on which the stars have not recorded their script. For
the stars inscribe the flow of time into the things of this world. And
Michael, the Sun Prince, rules the progress of time."

When the youth heard this, he felt the urge for action; he wanted
to become the defender of justice. "Master, I want to become a
grammarian," he declared. "I want to engrave a letter myself on the
cosmic script with my life."

In these sentences of Trevrezent, reported to us by Walter Johannes Stein, grammar becomes grand and broad. Not without reason, Rudolf Steiner indicated the importance of grammar in the Waldorf school curriculum. In discovering the laws of grammar in language, we discover the order that lies hidden in the outer appearance of the language. It stimulates to seeking for the ordering activity underlying the world of phenomena, while also bestowing on the practitioner of this art confidence in the world of observation. In turn, this awakens the urge to act. We feel real joy when we discover structures which at first sight remain hidden, but have been there all along, in every sentence. Love of language, the world of the word, grows and creates an inner 'skeleton' in the child's soul. It carries and forms the budding world of experience. Grammar is a real Sun Art, an art with which we want to work in the Waldorf schools.

In answer to the statement of the youth that he wants to become a grammarian, Trevrezent said:

"You will, because you are destined to do so and your ardour
will enable you to fulfill your vocation. Know then that the most
wonderful character is the bodily form. You will learn to engrave
the form of your future body when you pass after death through
the region of the sun to approach the sphere of Mars. Mars is filled
with activity. In its sphere you learn to draw the lines for future
development. It is the teacher of geometry. But it does not teach
tedious geometry; the lines it draws have to be conquered. Great
generals are geometricians in the heavenly realms before they
descend to do their deeds on earth."

The old man was filled with enthusiasm. He seemed to know more
about this region than about the others. But the youth had not
heard everything. He sat there pensively and said: "Love is stronger
than hate, isn't it?"

"It is so indeed," the old man answered.

"What does the soul experience in sleep?" the youth asked. "What
does it see when it learns to carry the light of consciousness into the
darkness?"

"It sees how the soul itself works to restore the body," the old man said.

"Is the soul then in heaven among the stars?" the youth asked.

"It is. It builds the body according to the archetypes in the stars. When your body lies asleep," the old man said, "the soul weaves golden threads from ganglion to ganglion. It draws triangles and all kinds of shapes from the star pattern."

"So that is geometry," the youth said, "and Mars is its teacher?"

"Of course," the old man replied. "You build in the blood according to the archetype of these patterns."

"God, then, is always engaged in geometry," the youth said.

These are deep secrets of existence that Trevrezent was telling his pupil here, but the pupil, in the awakening of his own forces, continually poses deepening questions, and in this process, the art of geometry becomes visible in all its facets. In Waldorf schools this art is practiced from the first day in first grade. Together with the children, with whom he will have an intense relationship for many years, the teacher draws the first geometric forms. These are archetypal forms: the straight and the curved. In creating the first forms as if he were drawing them, the teacher walks, step by step, a path which through many years of form drawing leads to geometry. Every week again, the straight and the curved are conquered anew in form drawing, and from sixth grade this practice finds its continuation in geometry. But most great is the world that hides behind this art! How instructive are the words of the old man!

"Now teach me the art of Jupiter. I have learnt to create forms which can serve living things. But where does life stream into these forms?"

"That happens in the realm of Jupiter," the old man said. "On earth you are aware only of life in the form of thinking. Thinking, and thus life, have their home in the sphere of Jupiter. It is the origin of life."

"But which is the art?" the youth cried. "Teach me the art of Jupiter."

"That is the art of speech," the old man said, "for rhetoric is the art of infusing the forms of Samael with life with the power of Zachariel. Mars forms the word in the air but Jupiter fills it with life. Zachariel, the spirit of Jupiter, teaches you to enliven your words so that joy and wellbeing stream from them."

The teacher uses this art in the class with the children all the time. His words want to bring joy and health. How difficult it is sometimes to find this vivifying force day in day out! But how deeply does it work when this power of the word lives in the class! Steiner worked intensively with the first teachers on this art of the word. He gave them many exercises so they could stand in a living stream of the word during their work with the children.

The last art is now mentioned by Trevrezent himself:

"Now there is only one sphere left," the old man continued. "It is the furthest one, Saturn. It is Oriphiel who embraces everything and forms its boundary. This is the sphere where the soul turns round after death. In the region of Mars the soul has refashioned the body to the form it should take in the next life. In the region of Jupiter it has prepared the new life which vitalizes the created form. Now in the sphere of Saturn, it ensouls its creation. In its descent to earth the soul will become filled with spirit and form, a new ego-consciousness. Then it chooses the time and place of its birth in anticipation of its descent. At that point the soul learns the art of astronomy."

Thus the youth learned of the last of the Seven Liberal Arts. What can this art give us as teacher and parent? Astronomy is taught from seventh grade in Waldorf schools. The world of the visible stars is then explored. But the Grail story also teaches us another way to approach the world of the stars. This is called the reading of the script of the stars. What is being read in this script? In this script those individuals are sought who one day will serve the Grail. The completely individual impulse with which each human child is born becomes visible in the script of the stars. This is precisely the riddle with which we are confronted as parent and teacher. And in our task we look for the solution. Here we work out of the script of the stars with a true astronomy that is transformed into the art of education.

The youth thanked the old man with the following words:

> "I thank you. You have taught me much because you have brought me true tidings of the seven arts that liberate the soul and the spirit from the body, which otherwise happens only in death. In life I learn to die and in death to live. The Seven Liberal Arts are one path."

20

EMIL AND BERTA MOLT'S ENCOUNTER WITH PARSIFAL

*E*xactly ten years before the founding of the first Waldorf school, Emil and Berta Molt were in Munich. Rudolf Steiner was giving a lecture cycle entitled "The Children of Lucifer and the Brothers of Christ." There was also a performance, created with great dedication, of a mystery drama set in early Christian times and written by the French poet Edouard Schuré. Interspersed with the lecture cycle Steiner gave two additional lectures about Parsifal in the framework of the Esoteric School. These two lectures were intended as meditation content for the participants.

In his autobiography Emil Molt described that it was of great significance to him and his wife to have been part of this Esoteric School since 1908.[89] From that moment they were able to follow the esoteric lessons Steiner gave for people who wanted to practice concrete exercises in meditation. Emil and Berta Molt were therefore present at the two lectures about Parsifal.

These lectures have been preserved in several different versions. Because nothing was written down during these esoteric instruction sessions, several participants wrote reports for themselves later from memory. Fortunately because of the different versions comparisons can be made, which make them into authentic reports of the material Steiner brought at that time.

For the Waldorf school movement the lecture about Parsifal is of great importance. Here Emil Molt not only became acquainted with Parsifal on an intimate basis, but he also heard how Charlemagne was related to the Grail mystery. Titurel, the builder of the Grail castle, is described as the one who inspired Charlemagne. In addition, Steiner spoke about Charlemagne as "the reincarnation of a lofty Indian adept." Thus Emil Molt heard about two aspects of the being and work of Charlemagne. He heard about Titurel as the inspirer of Charlemagne, and about the Indian adept as the individual karma of Charlemagne himself.

How deeply touched must Emil Molt have been when, ten years later around the time of the founding of the Waldorf school, Steiner subtly called to his attention his personal relation to Charlemagne.[90]

Berta and Emil Molt

The description of Parsifal Rudolf Steiner gave in these lectures is not intended as information that is interesting to know, but as content for exercises in personal meditation. Parsifal's spiritual path is described as an exercise that can be practiced by modern human beings. It is the exercise of the Grail seeker in the era of the consciousness soul. Steiner called Parsifal the pioneer of the consciousness soul.

For Waldorf school teachers the content of this lecture gives a genuine meditation content that can support their pedagogical work. The following is a rendition of this first Parsifal lecture given on August 27, 1909.[91]

> The old mysterious abodes of the Sun oracle exerted their influence
> in Atlantean lands. Their wisdom was transplanted into the post-
> Atlantean cultures. Two streams of people came forth from Atlantis.
> One went through Africa, preparing the later Egyptian culture,
> toward Asia, toward India and the East altogether, preparing for
> the Christ light. The other stream of people went through Europe

toward Asia and left part of the stream to settle in middle Europe. These people were led from the mystery centers, and the task of these centers was to prepare the West for the Christ light that was to come to it later. A strong race of people with strong physical powers was to be educated: Emotionally strong, courageous, the forces of the heart were to be trained; that was their striving.

Invisible to the people, great spiritual leaders from the spiritual heights guided this humanity and its mystery centers. One of them was the so-called Round Table of King Arthur, the others the Druid centers, the Trotten centers, the mystery centers of the Ingäwonen.[92] …In one region of Europe, in the west, part of this migration remained behind under a leader of whom we find a weak echo in history: King Arthur and his Round Table. At that time Europe had to be entirely prepared for his [Arthur's] later development, and special individuals were chosen for this purpose in order to organize the people so that they would be suitable for this later development. This was the first mystery school in Europe. Then came the age of Christ Jesus in the East. What ordinary history has to say about the moral and intellectual significance of these people is usually entirely wrong in the light of esoteric facts.

There are, so to speak, inspirers in the spiritual world for such leading individuals. Among them are two spiritual beings, whose names are only weakly conveyed in history as 'Flor' and 'Blanchefleur' [rose blossom and lily blossom]. These inspired, among others, Charlemagne. …Charlemagne, who came from the East—he was the reincarnation of a lofty Indian adept—was an instrument of the spiritual individuality symbolized by the name Titurel. …

During the age of the Mystery of Golgotha, a lofty individuality was withdrawn into higher worlds in order to bide his time waiting until the time was ripe for his special work. He remained away for centuries, and finally he came back as King Titurel, to whom the Holy Grail was entrusted, the cup that had been brought by angels from Golgotha to the West. …

The saga of the Holy Grail says that the cup with the collected
blood of Golgotha was brought by angels to Europe. Titurel
received this cup. He kept it hovering above the countries of
Europe, and only after centuries did Titurel descend with it from
spiritual heights down to the earth to found the mystery center
of the Holy Grail on the mountain of salvation [Montsalvat]. He
could do that only after several people were mature enough to
receive the secret of the Grail. Everyone mature enough for this
initiation was called Parsifal. …

The story of one such Parsifal shall be told. A Parsifal had
purified his soul of all earthly wishes and selfishness through long
meditation and concentration. He was a Cathar[93] and stood pious
and pure before his master Titurel who told him that all the forces
that Parsifal had acquired through his long years of meditation and
concentration were now to be used to fulfill himself. First he had to
sacrifice his intellect. In setting out to do this Parsifal strove with all
the power he had acquired through long exercises. He succeeded in
lifting up his higher I. He stood over and against himself.

Then he experienced what is written in the following esoteric script.
Parsifal saw his being as in a symbol. Before his eyes his physical
surroundings disappeared and were transformed into a picture
of a plant-tree, as big as the earth. It was full of rising fluids, and
a wonderful lily sprouted above as its blossom. When Parsifal
was immersed in beholding it, he heard behind him the voice
of Blanchefleur, who was symbolized in the lily, saying: "That is
you." [Then he knew that everything he had achieved through his
meditation exercises had formed the image of this lily. He knew that
in this lily he was seeing his soul purified of passion and desire.]

The lily was glorious and perfectly formed, but it sent forth a
strong aroma that had a repulsive effect on Parsifal. And it was
clear to him that this aroma symbolized everything he had set
outside himself through catharsis and that it now surrounded
him like an atmosphere. From this he understood that the lower
elements that he had set aside were not destroyed, but rather were
in the atmosphere around the lily. He learned that he must take all

that back into himself in order to transform this aroma from the lily. With this knowledge he watched the tree wither; the symbol disappeared and it got dark.

After some time another symbol arose out of the darkness for Parsifal: a black cross entwined with red roses. The tree transformed into the black wood of the cross and the fragrant roses, was created by the sacrifice of the life of the white lily. And behind Parsifal the voice of Flor, whose symbol was the strong, red roses, spoke: "That you will become." The aroma had disappeared; the roses had absorbed it. Parsifal saw that purification was not enough. He saw that he had to nail his lower self onto the black cross … and conform to the life of Christ; he must take it into himself so that the red roses would blossom. [He understood that the tree of life had turned into the dry wood of the cross, but also that this would enable the lily to be transformed into blossoming roses.]

…After this Parsifal went to a place of solitude and day and night let these symbols work within him. With time these symbols paled, yet the effects of their power remained and worked in him in the same way as the forces in a seed cause it to germinate and shoot forth. In the deep solitude in which he stood he looked around. He looked forward and backward, up and down, right and left. And he felt the great unity in everything. He felt the great enveloper, the all-encompassing one. And he felt how the all-encompassing one sent forces from all sides, and he experienced himself as a point, as the middle point, the center of these forces.

He felt that this point within himself would be part of the great enveloper. And he then felt from the one side a stream that flowed through him and pushed him to be dissolved entirely in the Godhead, in these forces of the enveloper. But from the other side a force came that wanted to lead him to keep his self. …Thus he felt from the one side a stream that flowed through him and strove toward complete dissolution in the Godhead, in the forces of the enveloper; but from the other side came a power that wanted to lead him to develop his own self.

And while these two forces worked on him he felt a third power that joined together the previous two and led him to the periphery of the enveloper. …

1. … a power that extends into us to which we must learn to devote ourselves entirely, a power that we also apply, though unconsciously, when we concentrate on an object. In contemplation we must find this power.

2. … the power that drives us to be entirely ourselves, to maintain our own self, which we also need in order to have enthusiasm, initiative for our life in the outer world.

3. … is actually a circle, a power from below, the power of the one who encircles. This power drives us to see all the joyful and sad experiences of life as existing around us, not in us. We recognize in it the power that works in the cosmos. It works in such a way that it also propels the celestial bodies around us, which also work upon us from the cosmos outside us. …If we come to know this power, then we can look upon what life brings us in joy and sorrow with composure. We know that everything arises from necessity; this is the driving force of the law of karma.

Parsifal had achieved these three powers. He devoted himself to them. Then, from left and right, there came to him, so to speak, supports under his arms, something like warm and cold wings. From the left he felt a supporting power that flowed into his left side, warmth created by spiritual fire; and from the right a power that was cool, bringing coolness. Then, in the region of the larynx he experienced currents from both sides. They came from the angel of light, who carried the spiritual light of wisdom to humans. He drew this spiritual light into himself. Then, with his spiritual ears he heard sounds from the world of the harmony of the spheres, sounds that made clear to him the purpose and destiny of the human being and of world evolution.

Again he tarried for a time. Then something penetrated into his head from above and a sum of forces flowed down through him. Here he experienced, flowing into and through his entire being, the power that the creator allows us to experience as the power of the Father, in such a way that we feel ourselves as a creation of the creator. And with the continuous expression of this experience Parsifal's own being grew over the whole in the form of a pentagram. He felt himself as the son of this Father. He experienced the truth of the Rosicrucian saying:

> *Ex Deo nascimur*
> *In Christo morimur*
> *Per Spiritum Sanctum reviviscimus.*
>
> From the Father God we are born,
> In Christ we die,
> Through the Holy Spirit we come to new life.

Parsifal had all these experiences when he stood in solitude before Titurel.

With these words Steiner concluded the esoteric lesson. Emil and Berta Molt experienced this. In Steiner's words both Charlemagne and Parsifal had been fully present. When ten years later, on the eve of the course *Study of Man*, on August 20, 1919, Steiner spoke about the virtues of the Waldorf school teacher and mentioned enthusiasm and initiative, Emil Molt surely remembered Parsifal's path. The content of this lecture is extremely effective as meditation content. As a Waldorf school teacher, I have the experience that it is valuable for our work and supports it. It supports us in our task to be interested in the world and to stand full of initiative in our work with the children.

The content of this meditation can strengthen our capacity for inner deepening, for contemplation, and the power of our interest in the world. For inner deepening is always nourished out of true interest. Meditation and deepening can then join like brother and sister with pedagogic/didactic deeds committed out of strong initiative. As Waldorf school teachers we can then stand more strongly in our destiny, while at the same time gaining in freedom. Titurel was Parsifal's teacher, but this great guide of humankind certainly strives to be our teacher also.

21

WHO IS THE HISTORICAL TITUREL FROM THE GRAIL STORY?

*T*iturel is the legendary builder of the Grail Castle. He is still alive when Parsifal arrives at the castle. Ludwig Uhland made a nice summary of the traditions about Titurel in his book on sagas and legends:[94]

> The Holy Grail is a vessel from which Christ nourished his disciples
> at the Last Supper. It is made of jasper, a precious stone through
> the power of which the Phoenix rejuvenates itself out of the ashes.
> Someone who is ill and beholds the Grail cannot die for a week.
> Regular beholding of the Grail bestows two hundred years of youth
> on the beholder. The same vessel was used by Joseph of Arimathea
> to collect the blood from the wounds of the Redeemer. In very
> ancient times angels brought the stone to the earth, and it was
> written in the stars that one day a blessed generation would be
> called to be its guardians.
>
> This generation is descended from the royal family of Senabor
> in Cappadocia [in Turkey]. Three of Senabor's sons followed the
> Roman Emperor Vespasian during his conquest of Jerusalem. One
> of them, named Berillus, married the daughter of the emperor and
> received France as his property, while the others received Anjou and
> Cornwall. They were all zealous propagators of Christianity. Berillus
> fought in Galicia and Zaragossa, and his successor Titurison, with
> whom Elisabeth of Aragon was married, was even more powerful.
> Titurison and Elisabeth made a pilgrimage to the Holy Sepulchre to
> implore God to give them a successor. There they offered a golden
> statue. Their prayer was answered, and in their joy they dedicated
> their child to heaven. An angel then proclaimed to them that their

child would be a good defender of the faith and would one day become a companion of the angels himself.

As a watchman after a long, cold winter night greets the morning sun … and as a lover greets her loved one, so heart-warming was the appearance of the handsome youth Titurel. Many women lovingly greeted him, even a hermit would have succumbed to him. But Titurel kept in his consciousness the proclamation of the angel at his birth.

In this text by Ludwig Uhland we find a reference to an area in the north of Spain (Aragon) in relation to Titurel and his family. According to the legend Titurel built the Grail Castle in this area, and this was confirmed by Rudolf Steiner:

It is not by chance that the temple of the Grail was supposed to be found in Spain, where one literally had to move miles away from what earthly actuality presented, where one had to break through brambles in order to penetrate to the spiritual temple that enshrined the Holy Grail.[95]

This is also the area that was invaded by Charlemagne after his defeat of the Saxons in 772, and where he conquered Pamplona and, to the great indignation of the citizens, gave order to tear down the city walls. The hatred he caused by this deed became the cause of the unexpected attack near Ronceval where Roland died. Later, Charlemagne sent another army to this area, now under the command of Hugo of Tours and Matfried of Orleans. This campaign also failed, this time because the army moved too slowly. Would this have anything to do with a certain resistance to go to this holy area of Titurel, where a form of Christianity was living that was free from Rome and had been there ever since the days of the Visigoths?

It is surprising to hear from Steiner that it was precisely Charlemagne who worked out of the inspiration of Titurel, while it was also precisely he who twice sent armies to this area, where Titurel laid the foundation for Grail Christianity. What is the secret behind Titurel? Which individuality is working here? He who, on the one hand, was an inspiration for Charlemagne and, on the other hand, laid the foundation for the Grail Temple?

While working on my book on Daan van Bemmelen,[96] I came across a quote from the same lecture by Steiner I have used in previous chapters about Charlemagne and Titurel. I was unfamiliar with this quote; it comes from the archive of Elisabeth Vreede:

> Charlemagne was for Titurel like an instrument in the outer world. Titurel's pupils were called Percevals. Titurel is the one who left at the time Christ descended to earth: the Zarathustra individuality. In the Grail is conserved the I of Zarathustra who put his three sheaths at the disposal of Christ. Only when he had left his body did he become completely permeated by the Christ. The images of this I are guarded in the Holy Grail and starting in our time they will become available to human beings. Titurel was able to appear on earth again when a number of human beings had developed to such a point that they could understand the Mystery of Golgotha. Parsifal was able to absorb this new knowledge.

This hitherto unknown version of the esoteric lecture of August 27, 1909, was not included with the other versions which are reported in *Esoteric Lessons 1904–1909* (GA 266/1), and it is the only version in which specific reference is made to the relationship between Titurel and Zarathustra. For me, this fragment made an unexpected connection between the theme of the relationship between Charlemagne and the Waldorf school impulse on the one hand, and on the other hand the individuality of Zarathustra.

When Parsifal became Grail King and assumed the task of Titurel, the builder of the Grail Temple, at that moment Titurel was able to die.

Daan van Bemmelen lived with the individuality of Zarathustra all his life. In Titurel we find this individuality again in the founder of the Grail mysteries. And Charlemagne was the one through whom Titurel could work into external culture. One of Charlemagne's impulses was the founding of schools for the people, public schools.

Just as in ancient Iran Zarathustra brought cultural life to combat brutality and devastation, in a similar way Charlemagne and his companions brought a cultural impulse in then still wild and savage Europe. In the process mistakes happened, such as in Pamplona and with the Saxons. And yet, it does look as if a great individuality was engaged in this germinal work in the sign of the Grail.

In this way the quotation given above from Steiner can lead us to develop a deeper connection with the impulse that proceeded from Charlemagne for the founding of schools in Carolingian times. It is the impulse of Zarathustra which came to fruition in Carolingian times, in a subsequent phase in the evolution of humanity. In our time this was continued in the founding by Emil Molt of the first Waldorf school in Stuttgart. When Steiner said that it is the good spirit of our time, Michael, who overshadows the founder of the school,[97] we can experience the blessing force of Titurel in inner continuity.

Zarathustra fought in ancient Iran and Iraq for a culture worthy of the human being. This involved him in a struggle against the materialistic impulses of Ahriman, who aims to harden culture and kill the creative spiritual power of the human being. In this light we may feel permeated by the earnestness of the spiritual task that stood, and continues to stand, behind the founding and the founder of our Waldorf school movement.

22

THE SUN CROSS MOTIF
OF FRITZ COUNT OF BOTHMER
AND FURSA OF PERONNE

*F*ritz Count of Bothmer is a name we all know in Waldorf schools, mostly because of the Bothmer gymnastics he developed. He devised a curriculum, starting in third grade, for a new art of movement that supports gymnastics. The movements in Bothmer gymnastics are based on the three spatial directions Rudolf Steiner discussed in relation to the human form in many lectures, especially in 1920. In rhythmical movement exercises Bothmer explores for every age group a new relationship with threefold space. He worked out of the Irish Sun Cross.

Fritz von Bothmer was born in Munich in 1883. Just like his father, who died young, he received training in the Bavarian army. He married Hildegard in 1913. In 1914 World War I broke out and already a few weeks later he was injured at his shoulder. A few months later he was back at the front in France.

> Almost every day I had enough quiet time to write a letter to Hildegard. And I was lucky to run into my friends Hans Strauss and Max Wolffhügel in Peronne. They were working there as volunteer orderlies.

It is striking that this first encounter with people who, just as he, were interested in anthroposophy took place exactly in Peronne. This place in the north of France, close to Amiens, is seen by researchers as a 7th century center of Irish-Celtic Christianity. Time and again we see here the name of the Irish-Christian initiate Fursa.

Who was this Fursa of Peronne?[98] He was born into a family of Irish nobility. Eventually he built a monastery in Ireland, with the blessing of his parents. One day while he was traveling, he was suddenly taken very ill. He lost consciousness and was brought to a nearby house. Today we would say that Fursa had a near-death experience during his unconsciousness. He experienced that he was accompanied by angels into heavenly spheres. He passed the four fires of trial and also saw the battle in heaven between angels and demons. He also met people who had died and whom he had known during their lives. Then he was called to return to his body in order to make the knowledge of a spiritual world known to the living on the earth. Thus he came back to the land of the living, and for twelve years he traveled around Ireland to speak about a spiritual Christianity and his own experiences in the spiritual world.

In the year 621 Fursa decided to cross the Irish Sea and go to England. In 641 he reached the continent of Europe. He made land by the rivers Marne and Somme. After his death an Irish-Celtic oriented monastery was built along the Somme; later it was called 'Peronna Scottorum.' His friends Foillan and Ultan worked there in memory of their great companion.

This is the place where Fritz von Bothmer ran into his two friends, and later colleagues at the Waldorf school. In Peronne they worked together with the contents of anthrosophy during World War I. Fritz arrived as an officer, and Hans and Max as volunteer orderlies for the thousands of wounded soldiers. Every day these three young men were confronted with the horrors of the war in the trenches where death was always waiting just around the corner. But in these dramatic situations on the borderline between life and death, many young people also had remarkable experiences that they later put in writing.

Count Fritz von Bothmer

In the 7th century Fursa worked with people out of clinical death situations. They told him of their experiences on the other side. He knew of those experiences because he had witnessed similar things himself. One day he was asked why he had a scar on his face. "A demon threw fire at me when I was passing through a certain area in the spiritual world after death. That demon clearly was still able to get at me!" was his humorous answer.

In the work of Fritz von Bothmer we see the same signature. He had been very close to death. His first injury took him to Hans Strauss and Max Wolffhügel. The second one, in March 1916, was a true threshold experience.

> In March 1916, I went back to France, to Verdun, not far from Rheims, where we became reacquainted with the war in the West. [He came from the eastern front. – FL] Here things became deadly serious. Chaumont-Douaumont-Fleury! As if you stepped into a very cold, no, a very hot bath. Verdun was nicknamed the 'great meat grinder.' No one went there with the illusion of ever returning. During the great offensive on May 23, 1916, I was lying prostrate on my face in a bomb crater. I had been shot through my face, neck and shoulder and was fully convinced that was going to be the end of me. I was saved by my faithful non-com, who since then was killed in Rumania. My wounds were dressed by the staff physician, who would be killed that same day.

> Only in the afternoon of the next day could I be carried out of the fire zone to Fort Douaumont. The intervening time, the night, and the trek to the fort belong to the most terrifying experiences of my life. That I ever survived remains a miracle to me.

Recuperation took a long time and was interrupted by life-threatening complications. However, despite these events, Fritz was fighting in Rumania again in 1917.

After the war he considered opening a bookshop. He and his family lived in abject poverty in 1922. He could not see a way out of the poverty and the degeneration in post-war Germany. But in March 1922 he wrote: "Since yesterday I am no longer an officer … I am a teacher at the Waldorf school in Stuttgart!"[99] He was soon asked to set up the physical education program.

> My soul forces are being sorely tested … the preparation for gymnastics and the gymnasium, the hard study of the new and incredibly profound pedagogical lectures by Rudolf Steiner … The school and all its problems … *I have to expand in my essential being so I can find room in my poor 'I' for all of this.*

He literally found this room in the exercises he developed. He was very modest and gladly shared his findings with colleagues, among them Nora von Baditz, Walter Johannes Stein and the school doctor Eugen Kolisko. These findings often brought up profound experiences that sometimes reached back into the far distant past, as in the following incident related by Walter Johannes Stein after Bothmer died in 1941:

> I was sitting in the teachers' room late one night after all my colleagues had finished their work and gone home. I was alone and immersed in the preparation for my history lesson of the next day. The door opened and Count Bothmer came in. "Working so late?" he said. "The others have long gone."
>
> I said: "Yes, I don't have everything together yet for tomorrow."
>
> "Tomorrow," he said, "it is already tomorrow." Then he said as if lost in thought: "What a different being you are than I am. With you everything becomes thought, with me everything goes into the limbs. I believe," he continued, "that I am a human being with Saturn qualities, for everything goes very slowly with me. It takes me a long time to come to results. And when they finally come, they are not thoughts but cosmic images which I take into myself reverently. And when I surrender to those images in reverence, then what I feel becomes gesture and pours itself into my limbs. You see, like this, for instance …"
>
> He knelt, curved his upper body backward and stretched his arms forward, one a little more and one a little less, but both forward and upward. "Do you see this gesture? It is the pattern of movement of the passages in the great pyramid and the path of the souls that loosen themselves from the body." It was an Egyptian priest who was kneeling there and said, with reverence on his face: "I have no thoughts."
>
> I went to him, took both his hands in my hands, gently pulled him up and said: "Have thanks, dear Count, have thanks." He left, and I continued my work.[100]

We see here an encounter of two human beings who, precisely in their differences, are able to experience each other as brothers. In their spiritual collaboration grew a mutual appreciation. It could have been different. For Fritz it was not always easy to find his way with the children in the higher grades. He demanded a lot of the students and sometimes they felt this too much as a strange discipline. Fortunately there were discussions with Steiner:

> That evening we had a meeting with Rudolf Steiner in which I spoke about my problems in the higher grades. He did not agree that these were due to my teaching, for the children came to the lessons with joy. All I was lacking was a certain light-heartedness in the face of improper behavior. Also, the different teachers approach the students very differently. What the Count finds improper, Dr. Stein thinks is brilliant. We should not underestimate the form, and it would be good to devote a meeting especially to this subject.[101]

It is extremely instructive to use these two encounters between Bothmer and Stein to take a look at our own situation in the college of teachers. Bothmer and Stein shared form and content, and carried each other in their search for a genuine art of education. They also asked each other's advice in the development of exercises and lesson material. That night in the teachers' room Stein saw Bothmer in his essential being. He saw the priest who accompanies the human spirit in the connection between body and soul. He saw an Egyptian wise man.

Fursa of Peronne was an Irish wise man and priest. The Irish looked for the origin of their wisdom in Egypt. There was an ancient tradition of seven Egyptian wise men who brought the Christianized Egyptian wisdom to Ireland. Fursa was one of the first to bring this Irish spiritual impulse to Europe. The school in Peronne, founded after his death by his friends Ultan and Foillan, would become the basis for the arrival of many Irishmen in the century that followed. It would lead to the flourishing of Christian wisdom at the Court School of Charlemagne.

Just as Fursa, as spiritual leader, laid the foundation for the connection of Irish-Celtic Christianity with the school impulse of Charlemagne, Fritz von Bothmer was the leader of the Waldorf school in Stuttgart in the difficult years between 1933 and 1938. He was the one who had to close the school by order of the Nazi government. But in this closing he preserved the impulse of the school so that it could be resurrected after 1945. He would not participate in this on earth, for he died in 1941.

On March 30, 1938, Steiner's death day, the school was closed by Fritz von Bothmer. The teachers could not and would not meet the demands of the Nazi regime any longer. Bothmer gave his last address. The following words typify his impulse and his being:

> On June 16, 1936, Emil Molt died. Threatening clouds were then already gathering over the school. Now lightning has struck. But the moment the clouds wanted to change into a sea of suffering and sorrow, a ray of light broke through and in the radiance of the rainbow sounded the jubilating cry: "The Waldorf school lives and will live!" We have experienced it in these weeks, and nothing can rob us of this experience.

> This house is founded in the form of a cross. Here, through the middle of the gymnasium and eurythmy hall goes the trunk. From the stage one arm spreads to the teachers' room, and the other one to the doctor's room. From this point, here on the stage in the center of the cross, Rudolf Steiner and Emil Molt spoke to the parents and students. Here we had our most beautiful celebrations. Here sounded and radiated the heart of the Waldorf school most brightly. The form of the cross is the foundation of this house. And in the name of Him who died on the cross and lives forever in the people who give Him a dwelling in their hearts, the heart of the Waldorf school will also live on![102]

23

THE RENEWAL OF THE HIBERNIAN MYSTERIES IN WALDORF SCHOOL PEDAGOGY

*T*he Hibernian mysteries were called by Rudolf Steiner the last 'great' mysteries. They were called 'great' because they encompassed the entire evolution of humanity. These Hibernian mysteries had their centers in Ireland (Hibernia), but also there were places on the European continent even as late as the 9th century where one could go this mystery way accompanied by an initiated teacher. Many of the Irish-Celtic Christians who, after Columbanus, visited the continent of Europe as Christian 'Knights of the Word,' went through the schooling of the Hibernian mysteries.[103]

Around the time when the influence of the Hibernian mysteries was dying out, the foundation of the Court School of Charlemagne took place. It is an important contribution of Walter Johannes Stein that he showed in his book *The Ninth Century* that there were important representatives of Irish-Celtic Christianity working at the Court School of Charlemagne. We must therefore realize that this form of Christianity had its roots in the Hibernian mysteries.

Now, what was the way these teachers at the Court School and their predecessors went? And how can this shed light today on our searching and striving in Waldorf pedagogy? The way that led to initiation in the Hibernian mysteries was a difficult one full of trials.[104] First the novice was brought into a condition of total inner doubt. This doubt arose from the desperation that resulted from the search for true knowledge of nature and the soul. During this struggle of the soul, the novice was left completely on his own. But the moment he wanted, in the depth of his suffering, to renounce all spiritual striving the teacher intervened. From that moment on the initiated teacher accompanied the novice on his way. On this path, human soul and world soul were gradually united in the Christ experience. In the following dramatic fragment I have tried to create an experience of this path of initiation.

146

Novice: Where am I? Nothing around me
Reality or mere semblance
Bark and leaf, stone and wind
What is it, where are you – spirit?
World full of outer appearance
Full of disgusting insignificance
Thou in rocks, water, wind and fire
Hear me, speak to me – this hour!
I avert my face
Away from this mute darkness
Not speaking – not being?!
O listen, still
Soul speak, speak friends' language
The far heaven friends
Ah soul, the silence lames
Open your darkness for me
Be still, listen!
No answer…
No heavenly voices…
No friends in the darkness
… loneliness …
Cursed untruthfulness!

Initiated teacher:

Come, friend, follow me
Though deaf and seeing but darkness.

Novice: *(entering a temple – darkness lifts. Two gigantic statues, left a woman, right a man)*

How strange how darkness flees here
How great, how powerfully great, forms
(approaching)
I touch, it yields, vacuous hollow
Deceit, an empty sheath – man?
(the other statue)

I touch, it crumbles to formless dust
Semblance – full of life – woman?

Initiate: Find your way between semblance and deceit.

Novice: Where – where, o master?

INITIATION IN THE TEMPLE CAVE

Teacher and novice: *(beholding)*
            Snow flakes are falling.
            Silence descends from heavenly distance.
            Rest returns.
            I, a woman, leave tracks
            In pure snow.
            Snow flakes are falling,
            Silence descending.

Teacher: See what you were,
            What you willed before birth.

Novice: That I was before I was born.

Teacher and novice:
            The blood, it beats, it thumps
            On my temples.
            The warmth of the summer land
            Wishes to tear me from myself.
            It propels me upward
            To the boundary where life spreads out.

Teacher: See what you shall become,
            What you shall be after death.

Novice: The spirit world I shall enter
            When the body falls away.

Teacher and novice: *(echoing in beholding)*
>   Death and life, they know.
>   Behold the statues, look at them,
>   Behold past and future,
>   Hear them and connect them,
>   Enter the middle in the – now –
>
>   Seek the Christ – Sun Spirit –
>   *(Novice beholding at the teacher's words)*

In the temple cave the teacher leads the novice to two grand statues in the forms of a man and a woman. The male statue is hollow and elastic. After every impression it resumes its shape. The female statue is solid and crumbles where it is touched. Every impression is permanent. The male statue is lighted from above behind the head, and down toward the limbs it is less clearly formed. The female statue is lighted from below and becomes less clearly formed toward the upper body and head. The novice beholds these two statues, and during his second visit he may also touch them.

In the beholding and touching, experiences arise in the novice that lead to true knowledge of the human being. In the after-effect of these initiation practices, the novice is brought to a conscious experience of the spiritual powers underlying the nerve-sense system and the circulation and formation of the blood. Both of these experiences appear to his spiritual eye in the form of imaginations. The nerve-sense experience that arose from the male statue calls up an imaginative picture of a winter landscape. The novice senses himself surrounded by cold, snow and rigidifying forces. The experience of the blood circulation calls up a summer imagination, but at the same time the novice feels in his body the dissolving, depressing forces of warmth. In the further course of this path of initiation the winter experience leads to a conscious beholding of pre-birth existence, while the summer experience brings an image of life after death.

At this particular moment of the Hibernian initiation, the connection with *Study of Man*, the course Steiner gave for the first Waldorf teachers, can be seen in all clarity. The lectures of August 22 and 23, 1919, look like a renewal of the Hibernian mysteries within modern pedagogical striving. In both lectures Steiner points to the life of imagination and the life of will. And he creates a direct relationship with the nerve-sense processes and the blood circulation. In addition, he shows in all clarity the relationship of the life of imagination with pre-birth existence, and that of the blood processes with life after death.

It is as if in these lectures we are permitted to tread the path of the Hibernian mysteries again, but now as Waldorf teachers, with this difference: The external images that awakened spiritual insight in these mysteries have now, for 21st century consciousness, been placed directly in the situation of the profession. In the encounter with the children we can take this path as teachers, and thus we renew the old mysteries. That which long ago was lived through in deepest secrecy may now be striven for in the openness of professional life.

The first teachers' meditation, which is directly related to this course, offers the meditative deepening of this mystery path. This meditation gives us the possibility to use the *Study of Man* course not only mechanically as a spiritual-scientific knowing in our profession, but to actually live the spiritual reality out of which Steiner spoke at that time as an inner quality. With this insight, let us follow the further way of initiation in the Hibernian mysteries, so we can discover which experiences must not elude us as Waldorf teachers.

When the pupil in the Hibernian mysteries had lived ever more deeply in the polarity of pre-birth existence and life after death, as these dawned on him in the experiences of the nerve-sense system and the blood circulation, a will to find the connecting middle grew stronger and stronger in him. Upon leaving the temple then, two teachers showed him the image of Christ, and he was told that it is He who connects the polarity experienced by the pupil.

In the same way we can, out of our meditative deepening in the nerve-sense and blood processes, direct our attention to the connection between these two polar opposite streams. We then look for the breathing, rhythmical element that wants to live as a healing impulse in all our education. In a healing, harmonious pedagogy we can again and again experience the working of the Christ. It is He who stands by us in our daily task, in our encounter with the becoming children. This deepening in the nerve-sense and blood processes gives us the possibility to find the Christ ever more consciously. He is the one who calls for a pedagogy in which art and science are fully connected.

That which was once sought in the great Hibernian mysteries for centuries down into Carolingian times, for the good of a Europe in becoming, finds its renewal in Waldorf school pedagogy as this lives in the hearts of teachers who are dedicated to this striving.

24

CAROLINE VON HEYDEBRAND
AND RUDOLF STEINER

BETWEEN EUROPE AND AMERICA

Caroline von Heydebrand was born in 1886 in Breslau (then in Germany, now Wroclaw, Poland) into a family of the nobility. Among a circle of nine brothers and sisters, she was the second child. When she was fourteen, the family moved to Osnabrück in western Germany, where her father became a high government official. In 1910 she began her studies in German literature, history and philosophy in Munich. When there, she came in contact with Rudolf Steiner, who suggested that she look into the work of the poet Novalis. In due course this led to her dissertation "The Pupils of Sais, A Fragment by Novalis." She also studied in Berlin and lived there in the same apartment building as Steiner.

Caroline von Heyderbrand

In 1913 she played one of the four gnomes in the fourth mystery drama of Steiner. But the big turn in her life came when she wrote a letter to Karl Stockmeyer on June 2, 1919:

> Please forgive me that I am writing you without knowing whether
> you can use additional teachers. I have always had the wish after
> finishing my studies to commit myself as best I can to the impulse
> of anthroposophy. When my brother wrote me about your
> founding of a school, I thought this might give me a possibility
> to which I can dedicate myself. I must, however, add to my great
> regret that my physical capacities are not very great due to my
> delicate health.[105]

In 1919 she received her doctor's degree based on her dissertation on Novalis. And she was invited to come and work at the first Waldorf school in Stuttgart. She was handed the largest class, with forty-seven students, and had herself the smallest figure. Her colleague Fritz von Bothmer described this as follows:

> Caroline von Heydebrand was in her thirty-third year when Rudolf Steiner asked her to come and work at the Waldorf school. Here she felt completely in her element, although the pedagogical work was also difficult for her. With her small, delicate figure she had to overcome some resistance to assert herself in the world. This means that it was a trial for her when she suddenly found herself in front of a large class full of eleven-year-old boys and girls. … Her capacity to realize what she observed in others, her readiness always to make room for greater impulses, her selfless will, the fire to gain insight, and the goodness of her heart, all this she united in her pedagogical deeds.[106]

She was able to work at the Waldorf school until 1938. Then suddenly the moment of departure from life came upon her when she was attending an anthroposophical conference in Bangor, Wales. The morning of her lecture in Bangor, the last one of her life, she climbed all alone, with all the forces she could still marshal, to a Druid sanctuary up on a hill. She also wanted to visit some megaliths in England. But coming back she missed the bus and had to walk for hours. Given her weak health this led to heart problems. After the conference she arrived with her friend Franz Loffler in Germany, and she died three days later.

Thus she gave her last lecture in Bangor, Wales. This was the place where Nennius wrote his *Historia Brittonum (History of the Britons)* around 800. Nennius—his Welsh name was Nynniaw—called himself a student of Bishop Elfod of Bangor. He collected many old traditions of early British history and geography. Thus he described as a historical fact that 'King' Arthur led his people in twelve battles, and that in eight battles at the fortress Guinnion he wore on his shoulder an image of Mary:

> Arthur wore the image of the Virgin Mary on his shoulders, and the pagans were scattered with great losses. … He fought the twelfth and last battle on Mount Badon.

In 1931 Caroline wrote a synopsis of the entire curriculum of the Waldorf school that was most useful when after World War II the schools could be opened again. And even now it remains a very helpful, concise and well-ordered summary of the whole curriculum.

In Bangor, around the year 800, in the time of Charlemagne therefore, there was a monk who wrote a book about a large part of the spiritual history of the Britons, thus preserving it from oblivion. The book begins as follows:

> I, Nennius, disciple of St. Elbotus, have endeavoured to write some extracts which the dullness of the British nation had cast away, because teachers had no knowledge, nor gave any information in their books about this island of Britain. But I have got together all that I could find as well from the annals of the Romans as from the chronicles of the sacred fathers, Hieronymus, Eusebius, Isidorus, Prosper, and from the annals of the Scots and Saxons, and from our ancient traditions.[107]

With these words Nennius opens his great book *Historia Brittonum*. His immense accomplishment and his contribution to our understanding of old history can hardly be overestimated. And if we were not already familiar with the ways of our own time, it would be hard for us to stomach the disdain he gets from modern scholars as quid pro quo for his work. His accomplishment lay in tracking down all available documents showing the origin of the Britons and collecting them in one book. It was a dangerous period for the Britons as a people and for the documents themselves. But for Nennius' effort, all of these documents would have disappeared without a trace.

The above translation (the book was written in Latin) speaks of the "dullness of the British nation." What is referred to here is the state of mind that followed on the mass murder of the monks of Bangor. The deep cultural shock caused by this murder of their finest scholars and spiritual leaders, perpetrated by supposed fellow Christians by order of none less than the Bishop of Rome, would leave a deep wound.[108]

This is the state of mind of the Britons (also called Welsh) which Nennius deplored and which caused the neglect and loss of many documents and books. 'They had no knowledge' because practically no one was studying any more.

Hence Nennius' sudden urgent collector's mania for everything that was left. He completed his work toward the end of the 8th century. His sources were numerous and varied. They also included parts of history Irish scholars told him about.[109] The place where Caroline gave her last lecture was this very Irish-Celtic monastery where Nennius wrote his Historia. The Irish-Celtic Christians also guarded the secret of the land in the West, America. They traveled to this continent just as the Vikings did. One of these travelers lives on in the Middle Ages in the story of "The Voyage of St. Brendan" to the isle of the blessed. Steiner mentioned this in a lecture he gave in 1917 in St. Gallen.[110]

Henry Barnes, the important pioneer for anthroposophy in America, relates the following regarding his encounter with Caroline von Heydebrand:

> I wanted to go to Stuttgart and learn about this new kind of education. We persuaded our parents to invite Dr. Roeschl and Dr. Lehrs to visit us in Stonington, Connecticut, so they could hear firsthand about this school. …On August 12, [1932] I celebrated my twenty-first birthday, inherited a thousand dollars, and, some ten days later, Edward and I were underway with doctors Roeschl and Lehrs, sailing for Cuxhaven, the port of Hamburg. Little did these two naïve young Americans realize the historical destiny into which they were entering.

> We were met at the boat by a friend of Roeschl and Lehrs, who we learned was a teacher in the Waldorf school. She was a small, feminine figure with a friendly smile, and keen blue eyes behind steel-rimmed glasses, her blond hair pulled back tight into a bun. This person was introduced to us as Fraulein Doctor Caroline von Heydebrand. As we drove through Hamburg, we passed a beautiful lake in that city's central park. There was a fresh breeze blowing and the lake was alive with white-crested waves. Both young Americans were native sailors and, especially the younger one was overwhelmed by a longing to get out on the lake and sail. To my great surprise, our older German companions asked us if we wanted to take a quick sail.

> The answer was immediate and unequivocal: "Yes, let's sail! Who would like to come with us?" The little lady who had met us as

we landed volunteered, and in a short time we were out on the lake, the sails billowing and the boat keeling to the wind. Our passenger glanced apprehensively from side to side as the boat careened in the stiff breeze and the waves dashed past the lee gunwale close to where she was sitting. Only much later did I learn that our passenger was perhaps the most distinguished member of the original Waldorf faculty, selected, trained and appointed by Rudolf Steiner himself. Thank God we didn't capsize, but returned Caroline von Heydebrand safely to shore. The readiness of these three pioneers of Waldorf education to humor the crazy whims of two wild young Americans is a tribute to their pedagogical insight and creative adaptability.[111]

Steiner considered Caroline von Heydebrand as one of the great pedagogical personalities in the school. Together with Ernst Uehli she wrote a children's book about stories from the Old Testament, and also the widely read book *Childhood* that was published by her colleagues after her untimely death.

Who was this remarkably modest, yet creative and carrying personality? She was convinced that she would be born again relatively soon so as to continue the work she had started together with her friends.

In 1922 she was in England together with Steiner who gave lectures on "Shakespeare and the New Ideals" at a non-anthroposophical conference on Shakespeare.[112] During this conference she spoke (perhaps together with others) with Steiner about the future. Steiner said something completely unexpected and also most hopeful. Caroline related the content of this conversation to a colleague at the school in Stuttgart, who then wrote the following brief note:

Caroline von Heydebrand said that Rudolf Steiner in Stratford-on-Avon in 1922 declared that he would return in eighty years in America.[113]

It appears that Caroline von Heydebrand is preserving impulses that have to do with the contact between America and Europe in past and future. In the time of Charlemagne contacts with North America were kept secret in monasteries such as Bangor. The purpose of these contacts was to arrive at new insights for the arts of healing and education, insights that could be found only on the American continent. Caroline was the first to receive Henry Barnes, the subsequent pioneer of anthroposophy in America, on the continent of Europe. She brought the young American into contact with the Waldorf school which can be seen as the breeding ground of a new healing art of education. In 1922 she heard words from Steiner that pointed her in the direction of the future in connection with America.

Since 2002 this future has become reality: More than the eighty years mentioned by Steiner have passed. Will Caroline again follow in Steiner's tracks in service of a healing art of education?

25

RUDOLF STEINER AND THE DESTINY OF THE WALDORF SCHOOL MOVEMENT

*T*his year it is 150 years ago that Rudolf Steiner was born. His cradle stood in the Croatian village Kraljevec where shortly before his birth his parents had moved from Austria. His father received a position with the railways there. Steiner said himself that it was not without significance that he was born there. He described how starting in the Middle Ages already Germanic and Slavic culture met in that area. What he did not say, but discussed with Ita Wegman and Walter Johannes Stein later, is that the place of his birth borders on the area that was described by Wolfram von Eschenbach in his Parsifal as the land of Gandin, Anjou (Parsifal, book IX, 499).

Through his grandfather, Parsifal is descended from the knights who lived there where the stream called "Grajena runs into the Drau." It is roughly the same area that was ruled by Duke Arnulf von Kärnten in the 9th century. The coat of arms of Gandin, Parsifal's grandfather, shows a black panther. A white panther on a green field is the coat of arms of Steirmarken in Austria. Parsifal inherited these lands.[114]

Parsifal himself was not aware of this, for his mother, Herzeleide, never told him of his origin. But there was a knight at the court of Herzeleide who knew it better than anyone. That was Schionatulander, a squire of Gamuret, Parsifal's father. Schionatulander was the one who brought the news of Gamuret's death in Baghdad to Herzeleide.

Steiner gave Ita Wegman the indication that he was karmically connected with this person, and she with Sigune. They had met at the court of Herzeleide and were bound to each other in deep love. Wolfram von Eschenbach spoke of the figures in the Parsifal story as historical personalities in the 9th century.

In this brief chapter in celebration of Steiner's day of birth, I will present a few aspects of his life as a knight over a thousand years ago. Schionatulander and Sigune were historical personalities in the 9th century.

They lived, unknown and unheeded, in a corner of Europe not without importance for anthroposophy, dying at an early age, but gazing for a brief moment as it were through a window into the civilization of the West, receiving impressions and impulses but giving none of any significance themselves. That was to come later. They had returned again into the spiritual world and were in the spiritual world when in the year 869 the 8th Ecumenical Council was held in Constantinople.[115]

Walter Johannes Stein concluded on the basis of the Parsifal text that Sigune's historical name was Elisabeth, because in saying goodbye to her Schionatulander calls on this name as a guardian power. In the 9th century it was custom to invoke the saint that was connected with one's baptismal name: "My departure is not inevitable; may God send you angels and may Elisabeth, the godmother of Christ, preserve you from suffering."[116] The 9th century began with the coronation of Charlemagne as Emperor. We have to look for Schionatulander in the time after Charlemagne's death in 814. Steiner told Ita Wegman that he (Steiner) died in the 9th century at the foot of the Hermitage in Arlesheim, Switzerland. "The connection between Dr. Steiner and me [Ita Wegman] lies in an incarnation in the vicinity of Basel. You [Stein] were at that time a hermit, a monk. The exact historical dates still have to be investigated." (Ita Wegman to Stein, January 6, 1925) Before he died on March 30, 1925, Steiner was able to tell Ita Wegman that the historical personalities behind Schionatulander, Sigune and the hermit Trevrezent are meant here.

That Walter Johannes Stein received such a concrete indication from Steiner as to his prior incarnation together with him and Ita Wegman in the 9th century was connected with the joint research the three of them were doing since 1923 as to the historical reality behind the Parsifal epic by Wolfram von Eschenbach. Stein then began his Parsifal block in the first eleventh grade of the first Waldorf school. Steiner had asked him to give this block, which connects so well with the development of the students in their seventeenth year. He had added the advice to Stein to investigate also the historical reality behind the pictures. During this block Steiner visited the class and worked together with Stein and the students on the lesson.

This joint research was to last more than two years. Not only did Stein find himself in the Parsifal story, but also his beloved friend and teacher. The figure of Schionatulander lit up in all clarity for him, and before Steiner died he was able to confirm this to him.

Who was Schionatulander? He was a knight but, according to Steiner, not very well known. He was Gamuret's squire, traveled with the latter to Baghdad, and died just like Sigune in 869, the year Steiner called the year when the 'spirit was abolished' within the threefold human constitution of body, soul and spirit, during the Council of Constantinople. Schionatulander lived in the first part of the 9th century. His task was to help Parsifal. Because of him Parsifal could take on the task of guardian of the Grail. Schionatulander and Sigune accompanied him on his way. Parsifal is there also today.

It was in 1924 that Ehrenfried Pfeiffer (1899–1961) asked Steiner whether Parsifal was on the earth at that time. According to Steiner that was not the case. He added that by karma his incarnation would be due by the end of the [20th] century, but that it would depend on the availability of Waldorf education and also on the manifestation of the Threefold Social Order. "Such an incarnation would bring about a complete change of trend in history."[117] The same goes for Steiner. Walter Johannes Stein wrote in his diary that in Stratford-on-Avon Steiner said in a personal conversation in 1922 that he would come back in eighty years in America. That means the year 2002.[118] We are now living in 2011 and are taking note of the year of Steiner's birth, 1861. In this chapter I most of all want to awaken our consciousness of Steiner as we can encounter him now again. It depends on our will whether a new collaboration can come about. The human being who wrote *The Philosophy of Freedom* will certainly respect freedom in a renewed acquaintance.

26

YOUR SCHOOL YEARS –
A PARSIFAL PATH TO ADULTHOOD

In the center of Holland, in the city of Utrecht, Rome-oriented Christianity was introduced in the 8th century by St. Boniface, the successor of St. Willibrord, who had previously brought the Irish-Celtic oriented form of Christianity to that area. With St. Boniface the Christian faith became more and more dominated by the rules and dogmas prescribed by the authority of the pope, while St. Willibrord taught a more personal faith based on inner perception and experience.

At that time the old Germanic (Frisian) villages continued to exist where the agricultural land was held in common by all inhabitants. The work on the land and also the experience of the divine spiritual world were embedded in the seasons. The course of the seasons gave indications as to the moral quality of the tribe. The priest could read this from the relationship of sunlight and shadow around the great stone columns and altars. Places of justice, where the so-called 'Ding' or 'Thing' was held, were of importance here. Moral development, administration of justice and experience of nature were still felt with great spirituality as integral parts of the course of the year.

We see a relationship here with the Irish-Celtic element, the form of Christianity that is based more on one's own experience and less on authority. It is in this area, in the town of De Bilt, that the first Waldorf school in this part of the country was founded. In the nearby city of Utrecht, the seat of the bishop and therefore much more Rome- and authority-oriented, it took much longer for a Waldorf school to come into being.

De Bilt is also the location of the Dutch State Weather Institute that issues the daily weather reports. The weather is becoming increasingly unpredictable because of human interference in nature and the cycle of the earth. Formerly, the weather reflected the moral condition of humanity, and out of this consciousness it is quite possible to stand fully in the problems of our time in De Bilt. The Waldorf school strives to be a source of healing in the problems of our time.

The theme of this chapter is "Your School Years—A Path to Adulthood." We can make an analogy with the waxing phase of the moon. The moon grows from a small sickle to a round disc that in all its fullness reflects the sunlight. We could also view the child in its development to age twenty-one in the light of the waxing moon.

In its first seven-year phase—from 0 to 7 years—the child is completely dependent on the enveloping life light of mother, father and immediate surroundings. Everything speaks directly to the child: materials, bearing, and invisible emotions and thoughts. The child is shined upon from outside but does not reflect—in contrast to the moon—and absorbs everything deeply.

In the second seven-year period the influence continues to come from outside. Then it is especially the sun influence of teachers and other adults who are examples. Through them the child receives soul nourishment as from an unquestioned authority. The world can then be experienced in its richness and beauty, and the child is beautifully surrounded by sun radiance.

In the third seven-year phase, from age 14 to 21, the light is tested and judged for truthfulness. The children's independence is now awakening and growing. Staying with our image, the moon has now taken the sun into itself. In the sky we see the full moon; down here the light is reflected. In the development of the child the sunlight that shines onto him from the adults is absorbed deeply. The images of the waxing moon and the growth to adulthood speak a similar language.

When we now take a look at Parsifal on his way to adulthood we see that in his first years he was completely protected by his mother Herzeleide. Are we not, as Waldorf school parents and teachers, all like Herzeleide? Do we not all try to protect the children, and does the world not pull at the children to go out and take dangerous roads? In preschool and kindergarten, and even in grade school, it is possible to let the child be the 'dear boy' as Herzeleide called Parsifal, but then inevitably we have to say goodbye. The world tempts and the ideals call.

After his encounter with the knights, Parsifal goes out into the world, be it that his mother dressed him as a jester. Young people now look for their own path. Parsifal meets a woman, Jeschute, and kisses her because his mother had taught him so. That meeting has consequences. Then he meets Sigune with the dead Schionatulander on her lap. He hears his name for the first time: Parsifal, which means 'straight through the abyss.' Then he comes to King Arthur's court and, after defeating and killing Ither of Gaheviez, the red knight, he becomes an Arthurian knight. Anger made him into a knight; anger because of injustice suffered made him defeat Ither.

When young people have received sufficient soul nourishment between the years 14 and 21, they are able to stand on their own feet. If they slept through their high school years, no love for life and world will dawn in them, and the first years of adulthood may remain sort of lukewarm, indifferent. Anger serves to awaken the individuality in the soul, which is the reason why Rudolf Steiner called anger the educator of the sentient soul.

It is in the development of the sentient soul that young people stand between their twenty-first and twenty-eighth year. In those years a conscious transformation of the high school years can take place, which can then become the basis of true freedom in the spirit. If universities were truly free institutions, they would be able to really serve this striving. When we are really free in our soul, we have the ability to shoulder responsibility. Before our twenty-eighth year it may be dangerous for our further development to carry too much responsibility. Our own identity does not yet have enough of a foundation in our own innermost being, and may be scattered outside.

In the time that then follows we are really on the Parsifal path in the direction of the abyss and the valley. We can have doubts, doubts about ourselves and our striving. We search for the truth. The search for truth, also concretely, carrying responsibility and looking for social structures in work and life, all this difficult. But Parsifal goes on; never does he stop.

In the period between 7 and 14 the children have taken in the truth of the world and its beauty through their teachers. This becomes the foundation for the development of the intellectual soul in a truly conscious way. Should this second seven-year period have been lacking in artistic work and sun-experience of the world, then the way through the valley can become really hard. It will demand much effort, and it all depends on the strength of the individuality whether the valley can be crossed. Thus we see that in the second seven-year period the basis is laid for the fifth period, that of the intellectual soul.

Then we come to our thirty-fifth year, about which the great Italian poet Dante wrote at the beginning of his *Divine Comedy*:

Midway life's journey I was made aware
That I had strayed into a dark forest,
And the right path appeared not anywhere.[119]

This is the beginning of the sixth seven-year period, ages 35–42. In this period we can review our first childhood again, but now out of consciousness. Parsifal goes through the deepest valley. His armor is rusty and closed; he is far from human warmth, from cities and family. But in this struggle he grows up in silence, and on Good Friday he rides into the forest and finds his way to Trevrezent. He drops the reins, he trusts in his horse to lead him to his destiny. He pays attention and responds to Trevrezent, the wise hermit who initiates him into the secrets of the Grail and leads him to self-knowledge. Parsifal recognizes his mistakes and in this way also finds his task again. Out of attention his true task is now born based on self-knowledge.

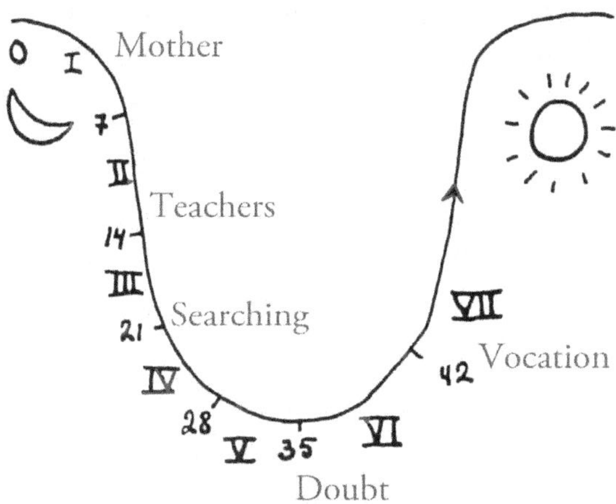

THE PARSIFAL PATH
1–7: Phases of Growth

It is the path we all go in our time, the path of the consciousness soul. In this mood Parsifal is able to bear his mistakes and yet continue to trust in the good. The foundation for this was laid in the first years of his life in the silent attention of his mother, Herzeleide. The good world of that time can now be visited consciously as the inner world. Now Parsifal is able to take on the task which is his true destiny. Of course, he has already done many things, but these came out of his own initiative. Now he is being called. He gazes at the Grail for the second time, but now he is called and knows what to do. Because of his own suffering, his path through the valley, he is now able to have compassion for the wounded human being and humanity. He knows to ask the right question of the wounded man, Amfortas, because of which healing forces become active.

In Parsifal appears the archetypal image of the human being who out of the conscious soul, the consciousness soul, has lived through and overcome individualism and can now attain to brotherhood. He now knows the distress and needs of his fellow human being, Amfortas.

Thus we see that the basis for brotherhood, the ability to recognize and respond to the needs of our fellow human beings, is laid in our earliest childhood years—from birth to our seventh year—by surrounding the child with the good. The basis of a real experience of truth in the conquest of doubt can be laid in the experience of beauty and trust in the school years between ages 7 and 14. This feeling for truth in turn becomes the basis for a true sense of justice. Lastly, in getting to know the world and our own soul, in the awakening of love for the world and the human being during our high school years, the basis is laid for the spiritual freedom of the now becoming adult human being. This spiritual freedom can be developed in many different ways at the beginning of adulthood in the fourth seven-year phase (ages 21–28). These might include traveling as it was done in the old days by young people during their years of wandering, or being a traveling journeyman exercising a trade, or engaging in free research at a university.

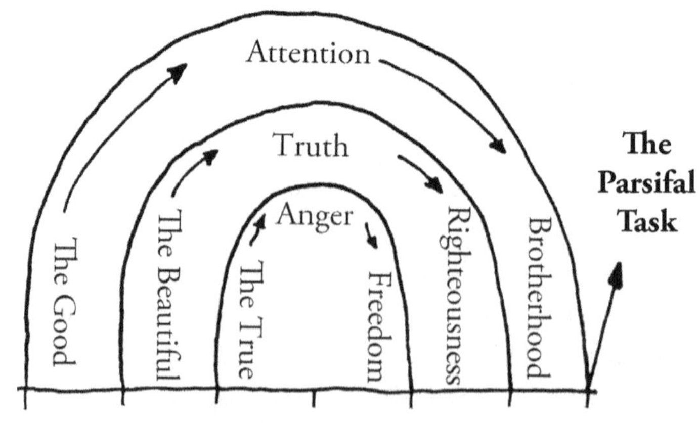

0–7: The good in the surroundings →   *attention* → →   *35–42: Deeds of brotherhood*

7–14: The beautiful in the human being → *truth* → →   *28–35: Sense of justice*

14–21: Truth and love for the world → *anger* → →   *21–28: Free spiritual life*

This fourth phase of life is indispensable for a free spiritual life. It is the truly free phase. It is precisely this phase in which our culture seriously fails us. This was the origin of the student revolt in Paris in 1968. Free spiritual life, true sense of justice and genuine brother- and sisterhood find their basis in the human being when he grows into adulthood. The school years must serve this growth into adulthood. Waldorf pedagogy aims to give the growing child what is healthy for each phase of development. Thus the child develops in the light and warmth of the sun. The Sun Community of the Waldorf school wants to serve this process.

27

HOW DO I FIND MY TRUE BROTHER?[120]

*I*n this chapter it is my task to consider our encounter with different world views, religions, and backgrounds at Waldorf schools. The Grail story can help us here.

Many studies have been made of the Grail, for instance, of the way Wolfram von Eschenbach described it in his *Parsifal.* Also the relationship to Islam has been examined, for instance, the names of the stars that are mentioned in his *Parsifal.* At the moment when Parsifal enters the Grail Castle, the stars are not mentioned by their Greek or Latin names, but the Arabic names are used. This has led many researchers to the conclusion that, although Wolfram called himself illiterate, yet he must have had deep insight into the culture of his time, also outside Europe. That was remarkable, for this story was told around 1200. Especially on the Wartburg, on the border between former East- and West Germany, this story was told by Wolfram every year anew. The story had many thousands of lines. Wolfram had a good memory; he could see everything in his mind's eye and tell it in living images. It was written down by someone else.

As becomes very clear in the story, Wolfram had great respect for what was happening in Iraq at the time. In the first part already Gamuret's travels are described: He goes to Babylon and there befriends the Baruch (the blessed one). There are people who think this was Al-Mamoun, the son of Harun-al-Rashid, because Rudolf Steiner pointed out to Walter Johannes Stein that Wolfram's words should be taken literally, that Parsifal lived eleven generations earlier. Figuring this from Wolfram's days, we arrive at a time around 870, the 9th century. The historical situation behind Parsifal, therefore, as told by Wolfram, played itself out in the 9th century.

We also know the 9th century in the context of Waldorf education. Our first adventure here is the course *Study of Man,* in the third lecture (GA 293, August 23, 1919) of which Steiner said:

In our teaching we bring to the child the world of nature on the
one hand and the world of the spirit on the other. In so far as we
are human beings on the earth, on the physical plane, fulfilling our
existence between birth and death, we are intimately connected
with the natural world on the one hand and the spiritual world
on the other hand. Now the psychological science of our time is a
very weak growth. It is still suffering from the after-effects of that
dogmatic Church pronouncement of AD 869—to which I have
often alluded—a decree which obscured an earlier vision resting on
instinctive knowledge, the insight that man is divided into body,
soul and spirit.

Wolfram had respect for the Arabic world, for the world of Islam, especially
for scientific, philosophical Islam that took a broad view, for at the court of the
Baruch astronomy was practiced. In his karma lectures Steiner gave an example
of an astronomer at the court of Al-Mamoun who later incarnated as Laplace.
Charlemagne also had no difficulties with the Arabic world. He received a
magnificent present, a white elephant, from Harun-al-Rashid, the great caliph
from *One Thousand and One Nights*. Charlemagne was greatly attached to this
elephant and had it brought to Paderborn.

In one of his first karma lectures, Steiner also said something about Harun-al-
Rashid, namely that we could find him again in Francis Bacon, the great founder
of natural science who coined the phrase: "When nature does not reveal her
secrets, put her on the rack." That was the beginning of our laboratory research.

Thus there was a highly developed culture in the Arabic world, and we must
make a distinction between Arabism, the Arabic world, and Islam. For it was not
always so that the caliph, the leader of the faithful, was strictly orthodox. In the
big cities in the 9th and 10th centuries, there was high culture comparable to
our time when people say that they are Christians. In Spain there were Moorish
hospitals, and if a visitor fell from his horse and broke a leg, he was looked after in
such a hospital. He was even given white (alabaster-colored) sheets. When he was
ready to be sent home, he received a note for medication from the pharmacy and
given a gold coin to make it through the first week.

In history education stories like this are increasingly appreciated. There are
more and more sources to approach, for instance, the Crusades from the point of

view of people in Jerusalem, comparable to the way the Afghans now experience that the Americans have come. The students find that extremely interesting.

At the same time when Wolfram's *Parsifal* was written down, Francis of Assisi was alive in Italy. He went to Al-Kamil in Egypt and walked there on fire, from which Al-Kamil knew: "I have found a brother here. This human being follows his heart and is sincere."

In modern history we also see people who have successfully dealt with the Arabic world, for instance Lawrence of Arabia. True, he worked for the secret service, but he was also able to live totally in the Arabic Muslim world, something he did indeed do in a most authentic manner. Eugen Kolisko, the first school doctor, once described that Saladin was Lawrence of Arabia's great example. Kolisko even sensed that Lawrence had an inner connection with Saladin. He wrote his famous book, *The Seven Pillars of Wisdom*, the seven pillars of the wisdom of Solomon, in which we can find the Muslims, the Islam. Suleiman or Solomon is for that people also a reality, just like Moses and Abraham are for theirs.

In the fifteenth adventure of the Grail story we find the Arabic world again, but now as it enters Europe. In total there are sixteen adventures. Walter Johannes Stein discovered that this number 16 is related to the development of the sixteen-petaled lotus flower, the throat chakra, and that in those stories the knightly virtues are a transformation of the eightfold path of Buddha. Going through the Grail story the traveler develops the right deed, the right habit, the right insight, and so on. These are the virtues Parsifal develops. And because besides Christianity he also took in Buddhism (Francis of Assisi was in reality also a Buddhist), he was able to transform the confrontation with the Muslim world into brotherhood.

And it is still a great secret that everywhere in the Grail story we meet elements of the Buddhist path of schooling which have been Christianized: the right insight, the right thought, the right point of view—Parsifal is confronted with this all the time. Have I come at the right moment? What do I do at the right moment? Do I speak the right word in the Grail Castle? It is the path the Buddha inaugurated around 500 BC but which is now being incorporated into the consciousness soul. Steiner said that around 500 BC Buddha gave the path of development for the consciousness soul, the eightfold path.

What do we learn on the eightfold path? We learn to prevent suffering, or to resolve suffering. Buddha called it 'to heal our karma.' For Buddha nirvana did not mean: 'I don't need to go back to the earth.' Nirvana meant that karma does not throw up new problems any longer, but takes us to the future.

The entire Parsifal story is filled with this theme. That is why the first thing Wolfram describes in chapter 1 is how Gamuret, Parsifal's father, arrives in Arabia and sees a city with sixteen gates which is being attacked. What he sees there is really his own throat chakra. And there is a virgin who needs to be protected. The throat, this Mars organ, must not always be talking, but must also be able to hear the words of the other. It has to become a flower that can receive the butterfly. That is the way Steiner also described this chakra. He said that if the chakra is properly developed it becomes like a flower that is moving.

And shooting through us are messages from the cosmos, like butterflies. In the forehead these are images, in the throat chakra they are more like words. A well-developed chakra is able to receive those butterflies for a moment. The butterfly can momentarily land and then we can hear or see it. Then it flies off again. If an imagination remains for a longer time, we know it comes from Ahriman. First Gamuret has to learn that, and then Parsifal. He does something with the path of Buddha and the Christian element in order to be able to meet Islam, to get to know the Arabic world better.

In the fifteenth chapter we have the final trial. Parsifal is called to the Grail Castle. He has met his double. For he has done everything wrong. He is like a twelfth grader who thinks: "Everything is going wrong." And suddenly things turn around and everything is going right. He rides out and then it is described how a knight lands in a ship. This is the 'fire son' Feirefiz. He comes from the south in search of his true brother and of his fatherland, the place he came from. He knows that his father is in Europe, but he does not really know him. And then what happens! These two ride up to each other, Parsifal dressed in red, Feirefiz in green, and they meet. The red man and the green man.

That could be a picture of the encounter with Islam when we realize what the color green means in Islam and that the red color is the blood of Christ and the red rose. If the Christ power is not carried outwardly as faith, but is taken inwardly, then the human being who was also called a Rosicrucian, or Grail Brother, is always connected with the inner red element.

Parsifal and Feirefiz meet and do not make way for each other. That is something I often stop to consider in class: "If you meet someone in a narrow alley, how do you manage that?" There are people who think: "O my God, there is someone coming this way. I am not here." Others say: "I am here!" Some people will pass each other and exchange a brief greeting. But these knights meet in a way that is an immediate invitation for battle. So, they fight.

Then we hear about Feirefiz's armor, which was made of precious stones in Arabia and was forged by fire spirits, by salamanders. He is therefore strongly connected with the elemental world. Salamanders are young elemental beings, young but very fiery and forceful. Having always lived in the desert, this knight Feirefiz has always had to deal with the fire element on the one hand and the moon sickle on the other. In the south the day is really the enemy of the human being, for it means heat. In the night the mild moon is shining. Thus Feirefiz was a human being who had lived strongly in moonlight.

He is described as having received a shield from his beloved made of a kind of wood called asbestos. That is said with great pride. In the center of the shield shines a carbuncle. There is also a carbuncle on the top of the Grail Castle, but here the carbuncle is lodged in asbestos and has a name. We might expect some kind of Grail name, but the name is: Anthrax. That touches me deeply when I think of all those letters with powder that were being sent around 9/11. Then we heard the word *anthrax* all the time, but here it is the name of that which Parsifal meets as a carbuncle that has a relationship to the Grail. You wonder why that name sounded so often around 9/11. Was that also a question after the Grail Castle? Where is our true brother? Who are we fighting really?

Parsifal and Feirefiz fight, and Parsifal strikes with his sword the top of the helmet of Feirefiz. Right there, on the top of that helmet, where other knights have a kind of emblem, sits a small being named Ecidaimon. In the Wartburg stories the Ecidaimon is called the being that represents the higher I of the human being, the I-daimon. Wolfram adds that this Ecidaimon is capable of destroying fifty poisonous snakes. That makes us think that it is a kind of being. Right next to that spot Parsifal hits the helmet of Feirefiz, and then his sword breaks.

At first I always thought that it was his Grail sword that broke, because he had received that sword in the Grail Castle. But later I realized that Wolfram says very clearly that this is the sword of the red knight Ither of Gaheviez whom Parsifal killed in a rage without realizing what he was doing. He knew that when he killed a knight he could have the armor. Thus he put on the armor and took the sword.

So this was the sword that broke. That with which his story began, with which he accumulated guilt, which he realized in his conversation with the hermit Trevrezent, is now totally lost, every step he made in his biography, his first steps on the way toward knighthood. To make a comparison, in the same way our first years in a Waldorf school throw their weight onto the last years. Once we received our sword somewhere, we probably experienced conflicts, and these return when we face a great task. That is what we read in Wolfram's work. For Parsifal stands here in a world moment, in the encounter with the Muslim-Arabic world. Now he suffers for all that went wrong in the beginning.

Then Parsifal does something extraordinary. He says: "Go ahead, kill me." He surrenders. That which gave him his name, his sword, his I, breaks and he surrenders and says: "Kill me." But before Feirefiz opens his visor, he says: "I do not kill unarmed knights." In the Arabic, Muslim world that is the standard. Also for the people I have mentioned, such as Suleiman and Al-Kamil, it was the standard that as noble human beings, they engage in honest fight, and if something like that happens, they do not go for the victory. Unlike what happens in the stock exchanges: When the prices drop, we rush to realize our profits.

That is a precious moment: the meeting between the Arabic world and the human being who has interiorized the Christ mysteries. For Parsifal is now worthy to become Grail King. He is on the way, in fact. In the moment when he loses he is able to say: "It is so," in other words "It is as God wills." He does not say that, he does it. And because he does this, something opens not only in him, but also in the other.

I am convinced that this is the greatest strength a human being can produce: that when you are attacked you open yourself and say: "It is so, it is as God has willed it." What Parsifal is about to experience then is: "Where two are gathered in My name …" That is literally happening at different levels. The moment they open the visors of their helmets, they discover in each other's faces the traits of their common father. And just in the encounter with Islam, Judaism and Christianity we always have the question: What is the relationship of the Son to the Father? Is the Father manifested in the Son? Or is the Son merely a prophet, a messenger of the Father?

The extraordinary thing here is that in each other's face they recognize the traits of Gamuret, who is the father of them both. And in the same moment something else happens: They understand each other. A higher union is forged; they find themselves in the same spiritual reality. "Where two are gathered in My name, I shall be in the midst of them." There the Son is present.

Parsifal has to bring a true brother with him to the Grail Castle, and Feirefiz is now invited to this. It is the greatest sin against the father in a Christian sense to go a path of initiation to the end without taking a brother along. It is the last trial Parsifal has to go through: He must take a brother with him. He has found his physical brother, but also his true brother, with whom he really has a much greater Father in common.

Then they go to the Grail Castle, and there twenty-five maidens, twenty-four plus Repanse de Schoye, bring in the Grail, a green stone, with the color that is so much part of the world Feirefiz knows. Wolfram describes how Feirefiz sees the carrier of the Grail; he sees her soul and her beauty. He sees her true stature, but the Grail itself he cannot see.

That is for me an interesting question. He does not see the Grail, and Wolfram says that the reason is that he has not been baptized; he is a heathen. When the teacher brings that into the eleventh grade, this is an exciting point, and it will raise an immediate question.

The interesting thing is that Feirefiz has also brought something with him. Repanse de Schoye is surrounded with the Grail by twenty-four lights. That is an inner space. Of Feirefiz we are told that he has come with twenty-five armies, all different armies that do not all understand each other. There are Saracens and Arabs among them. This raises the question whether he is fully Muslim, especially because it is mentioned that he is a heathen. He represents also the Arab world. He brings twenty-five from outside, and in the Grail Castle there are twenty-five on the inside. And in the conversation after Parsifal has been proclaimed Grail King, Feirefiz says that he cannot see the Grail, but he can see the carrier of the Grail.

And then something remarkable happens in this fifteenth chapter. It is precisely Repanse de Schoye, the carrier of the Grail, who enters into a relationship with Feirefiz, for it turns out that his first wife has died. Together they go back to Arabia, so that the Grail arrives in the Arabic world. Feirefiz does get baptized. Baptism is the act of purification from original sin, in a certain sense a return to our original state before the expulsion from paradise.

In a lecture Steiner said that the concept of Jesus in the Koran is most closely related to the child described by Luke, the Nathan Jesus. In 1913 Steiner gave the lecture cycle "Christ and the Spiritual World—The Search for the Holy Grail,"[121] in which he often mentioned the working of the Luke Jesus child, the pure soul of Adam, in the history of humanity. The deeds of this Luke child saved humanity from having to move over the face of the earth like animals, that we are not chaotic in our thinking, feeling and willing, and that we are not victims of all kinds of strong desires, but can speak. These were Grail sacrifices made by the Nathan Jesus being.

Then Steiner said that this Nathan Jesus being is the mystery of the Grail. The pure child that was born in a manger, this being goes through human history and makes sacrifices again and again. And it always raises itself again out of the ashes, always bestows itself again on humanity, but also always becomes the carrier of the Christ being again. In the Arabic world—and this started in Heliopolis in Egypt, near Cairo—this is called the Phoenix. It is the being that always rejuvenates itself by sacrificing itself, by opening itself to carry the Christ being.

This brings us very close to what was said earlier about the three Js: Judaism, Jesus, Islam. If we can open the J of our Jesus faith—let's just call it that for now—and can make the sacrifice to recognize that not just our Jesus religion counts, but what counts is that our Jesus concept opens itself to the Christ being, then the Christ being can come alive and work in the sheath of the Jesus being. One could say that the Jesus being is really the archetypal human in each of us, the part of us that did not go through the fall into sin.

This is brought to us every year in the Oberufer Christmas play. When we kneel by the manger there is something there that we cannot see, but we sense it: Here is a part of me that is pure. Young children do see the child in the manger. This archetypal human image is carried by Repanse de Schoye and Feirefiz into the Arabic world. I believe that Parsifal and Feirefiz learn to fulfill the archetypal image of the human being in themselves and also in the other.

ENDNOTES

1. At that time, schools did not yet exist in Europe, except in monasteries where teaching took place only in Latin, and mostly for clerical purposes. Kings and rulers could not read or write. [Trans.]

2. Rudolf Steiner, *The European Mysteries and Their Initiates*, lecture of May 6, 1909, from GA 57.

3. Rudolf Steiner, *Study of Man*, GA 293; *Practical Advice to Teachers*, GA 294; *Discussions with Teachers*, GA 295.

4. W.J. Stein, *The Ninth Century*.

5. W.F. Veltman, *Tempel en Graal (Temple and Grail)* about the karmic past of W.J. Stein.

6. See note 2.

7. From Johannes Tautz' biography of W.J. Stein. For instance, Rudolf Steiner typifies Alcuin as an Aristotelian (*The New Spirituality and the Christ Experience,* GA 200, first lecture).

8. Rudolf Steiner, *Esoteric Lessons 1904–1909*, GA 266/1 page 427. We have to realize that Emil and Berta Molt were present at this lesson (Munich, August 27, 1909). See also Emil Molt's autobiography.

9. Rudolf Steiner, *The Mission of the Individual Folk Souls*, lecture of June 12, 1910 evening.

10. Rudolf Steiner, *Esoteric Lessons 1904–1909*, GA 266/1, page 431.

11. Ibid., page 428.

12. Rudolf Steiner, *The Driving Force of Spiritual Powers in World History*, GA 222, lecture of March 18, 1923.

13. Rudolf Steiner, *The Mission of the Individual Folk Souls*, GA 121, lecture of June 12, 1910.

14. Rudolf Steiner, *Education as a Social Problem*, GA 296.

15. See chapter 3.

16. Husemann/Tautz, *Der Lehrerkreis um Rudolf Steiner (The Circle of Teachers around Rudolf Steiner)*.

17. An assembly of representatives of the people, mostly nobility and clerics.

18. Rudolph Wahl, *Karel de Grote, vader van Europa*, Amsterdam 1981.

19. A. Hausmann, *Kreis, Quadrat und Oktogon Struktur und Symbolic der Aachener Kaiserpfaltz*, Aachen 1994.

20. From Peter Godman, *Poetry of the Carolingian Renaissance*.

21. Ernst Bindel, *Die Geistige Grundlagen der Zahlen*, Stuttgart 1980: *Wen Christus wieder zum Leben gebiert, der wird in die Achtheit versetzt.*

22. From Peter Godman, *Poetry of the Carolingian Renaissance*.

23. Christof Wiechert in Frans Lutters, *Daniel van Bemmelen 1899–1982*, Driebergen 2005.

24. Rudolf Steiner, *Europäische Mysterien und ihre Eingeweihten*, GA 57, lecture of May 6, 1909 (not available in English).

25. Rudolf Steiner, *Background to the Gospel of St. Mark*, GA 124, lecture of June 10, 1911.

26. A.G. Weiler, *Willbrords Missie*, Hilversum 1987.

27. See Walter Johannes Stein, *The Ninth Century*.

28. Within the intimate circle of the Esoteric School, Rudolf Steiner often indicated that in Christian Rosenkreutz we can recognize the individuality of St. John the Evangelist. See also Bernard Lievegoed, *The Battle for the Soul.*

29. And of all Waldorf schools in the world. [Trans.]

30. The Latin word *flor* means *flower.* [Trans.]

31. Herbert Hahn, *Rudolf Steiner, Wie ich ihn sah und erlebte (Rudolf Steiner, How I Saw and Experienced Him)*, Stuttgart 1990

32. Phillip Heber, *Karl des Grossen geistlicher Rath und die älteren Waldenser, (The Spiritual Advisor of Charlemagne and the Elder Waldensians)*.

33. Schönhuth, *Chronicle of the Monastery of Reichenau.*

34. Phillip Heber, *Kaiser Karl des Grossen geistlicher Rath und die älteren Waldenser*, Basel 1857.

35. Ibid.

36. Saxnot was the name of the tribal god of the Saxons. Together with Donar, Wotan and all "evil spirits who are their henchmen," Saxnot had to be foresworn by Saxons when they were baptized. That Widukind called out the name of Saxnot in the church of Charlemagne means that he recognized his tribal god in the risen host.

37. J. Tautz, *W.J. Stein, A Biography*, Temple Lodge 1990.

38. Alexander Strakosch, *Lebenswege mit Rudolf Steiner*.

39. Rudolf Steiner, *Esoteric Lessons 1904–1909*, GA 266/1, page 443.

40. Alexander Strakosch, *Lebenswege mit Rudolf Steiner.*

41. The lecture forms part of Rudolf Steiner, *Wege zu eine neue Baustil*, GA 286.

42. Alexander Strakosch, *Leben und Lernen im Zeitalter der Technik.*

43. Wolfram von der Steinen, *Notker der Dichter und seine geistige Welt*, Bern 1948.

44. Ibid.

45. Erika Belte's memoirs from the German periodical *Mitteilungen*.

46. G. Husemann & J. Tautz, *Der Lehrerkreis um Rudolf Steiner (The Circle of Teachers around Rudolf Steiner)*, Stuttgart 1977.

47. Rudolf Steiner, *Esoteric Lessons 1904–1909*, GA 266/1, page 432.

48. Rudolf Steiner, *The Mysteries of the East and of Christianity*, GA 144, lecture 4, February 7, 1913.

49. Wolfram von Eschenbach, *Parzival*, Book III.128, translated by Mustard & Passage.

50. Rudolf Steiner, *From the History and Contents of the First Section of the Esoteric School 1904–1914*, GA 264, page 227.

51. Thomas Meyer, *Ein Leben für den Geist, Ehrenfried Pfeiffer (1899–1961) (A Life for the Spirit)*, Basel 1999.

52. Ehrenfried Pfeiffer, *Notes and Lectures Compendium 1*, Mercury Press, lecture of December 22, 1946.

53. The *Annales Fuldenses* are a record of history covering the years 840–901. They were written by several persons in the monastery of Fulda. They are an important historical source but are not objective since they were written from the point of view of the reigning rulers or of the authors.

54. Noricum was a vassal state of the Roman Empire in the area of present-day Austria.

55. Alemania (Latin) was a large part of present-day Germany.

56. Thuringia is an area in central Germany.

57. Saxony is an area in northern Germany.

58. R. Buchner, *Briefe des Bonifatius (Letters of Boniface)*.

59. Another anonymous chronicle of history.

60. An assembly of representatives of the people, mostly nobility and clerics.

61. Another anonymous contemporary chronicle.

62. At the Council of Constantinople in 869 the Catholic Church declared that the human being consists of only body and soul, thereby 'abolishing' the human spirit.

63. W. Delius, *Geschichte der irischen Kirche (History of the Irish Church)*, Munich/Basel 1954.

64. J. Streit, *Sun and Cross*, Floris Books, 1977.

65. The southernmost Austrian state situated in the Eastern Alps.

66. State in southeast Austria.

67. From J. Vermeulen, *Over Christelijke Heersers (About Christian Rulers)*.

68. Rudolf Steiner, *The Mystery of the Universe*, GA 201, lecture of May 16, 1920.

69. Ibid.

70. Emmy Matthes, secretary of the archive established by Walter Johannes Stein and Eugen Kolisko, helped Stein with his books until his departure for England in 1932. She wrote the following in a letter: "Before his departure for England, Dr. Stein said to me that he had wanted to dictate the second volume of *The Ninth Century* to me, because he was going to need it at the end of the century."

71. Rudolf Hauschka, *Wetter-leuchten einer Zeitenwende*, Frankfurt 1966.

72. Ibid.

73. See chapter 3.

74. Walter Matthes, *Corvey und die Externsteine*, Stuttgart 1982.

75. Widukind von Corvey, *Res Gestae Saxonicae (History of the Saxons)*.

76. Walter Johannes Stein, *The Ninth Century*.

77. Rudolf Hauschka, *Wetter-leuchten einer Zeitenwende*, Frankfurt 1966.

78. Ibid.

79. Ibid.

80. Ibid.

81. 'Smoking jacket' is a customary term for an 'alternative type of formalwear' in many countries in Europe.

82. Rudolf Hauschka, *Wetter-leuchten einer Zeitenwende*, Frankfurt 1966.

83. Bernard McGuin & Willemien Otte (editors), *Eriugena East and West*, Notre Dame, IN, 1994.

84. Letter from Daan van Bemmelen to Werner Greub in possession of F.L.

85. Chapter 16 of Walter Johannes Stein, *The Death of Merlin*.

86. This is the nickname Albrecht von Scharfenberg gives Trevrezent in his Grail epic *Titurel*.

87. See chapter 10. Waldo von Reichenau also received a blood relic for Charlemagne; it is still preserved on the island of Reichenau in Lake Constance.

88. Walter Johannes Stein, *The Death of Merlin*, Floris Books 208, chapter 16.

89. Emil Molt, *Entwurf meiner Lebenbeschreibung*, Stuttgart Freies Geistesleben 1972.

90. See chapter 2.

91. Rudolf Steiner, *Esoteric Lessons 1904–1909*, GA 266/1, SteinerBooks 2007. This rendition, created by Daan van Bemmelen, combines elements of records B and C presented in the book.

92. The Ingäwonen were one of the principal groups of Germanic tribes; they lived along the North Sea coast.

93. The word *Cathar* is related to *catharsis*, purification. [Trans.]

94. Ludwig Uhland, *Werke in vier Banden, Mit einer Einleitung von Dr. Rudolf Steiner (Works in Four Volumes with an Introduction by Dr. Rudolf Steiner)*, Weichert Verlag Berlin.

95. Rudolf Steiner, *Materialism and the Task of Anthroposophy*, GA 204, lecture 5, April 16, 1921.

96. Frans Lutters, *Daniel Johan van Bemmelen 1899–1982 Opnieuw geboren aan het begin van het Lichte Tijdperk (Daniel Johan van Bemmelen 1899–1982 Reborn at the Beginning of the Age of Light)*.

97. Rudolf Steiner, *Study of Man*, GA 293, first lecture.

98. Eleanor Shipley Duckett, *The Wandering Saints*, London 1959.

99. Fritz von Bothmer, *Die Biographie in Selbstzeugnissen; zusammengestellt von Alheidis Gräfin von Bothmer (Biography in Self-Testimony, Collected by Alheidis Countess von Bothmer)*, Stuttgart 2003.

100. Husemann & Tautz, *Der Lehrerkreis um Rudolf Steiner (The Circle of Teachers around Rudolf Steiner)*.

101. Ibid.

102. From a mimeographed copy of Bothmer's last address.

103. On March 22 and 23, 1924, Rudolf Steiner spoke in this connection about a prior incarnation of the Italian freedom fighter Garibaldi (*Karmic Relationships, Volume I*, GA 235).

104. Rudolf Steiner described this way in detail in *Mystery Knowledge and Mystery Centres*, GA 232, lectures of December 7, 8, 9, 1923; *World History*, GA 233, lecture of December 27, 1923; and *Cosmosophy Vol. 1*, GA 207, lecture of September 23, 1921.

105. Margrit Juneman, *Der Winter weicht; Caroline von Heydebrand (The Winter Fades; Caroline von Heydebrand)*, Stuttgart 2003.

106. Husemann & Tautz, *Der Lehrerkreis um Rudolf Steiner*, Stuttgart 1977.

107. From fordham.edu/halsall/basis/nennius-full.html.

108. Rev. Theophilus Evans, *The Primitive Ages*, Edinburgh 1834. This event occurred in 601 when the Saxons murdered twelve hundred teachers and students of the monastery school in Bangor. Even today many Welsh historians see in this the hand of Rome against a center of Irish-Celtic Christianity. Pelagius, the great proponent of free will, and strongly opposed by St. Augustine, came from this school in Bangor.

109. Bill Ashford, *After the Flood*, Middlesex 1995.

110. Rudolf Steiner, *Geographic Medicine*, lecture of November 16, 1917, from GA 178.

111. Henry Barnes, *Into the Heart's Land*, SteinerBooks 2005, page 192.

112. Rudolf Steiner, *Waldorf Education and Anthroposophy, Vol. 1*, GA 304, lecture of April 19, 1922.

113. The colleague was Walter Johannes Stein who wrote it in his diary, with the result that it was not lost. See Ehrenfried Pfeiffer, *Ein Leben für den Geist 1899–1961 (A Life for the Spirit)* introduction by Thomas Meyer, Basel 1999.

114. See Walter Johannes Stein, *The Ninth Century*.

115. Rudolf Steiner, *Karmic Relationships, Volume VIII*, lecture of August 14, 1924.

116. See Walter Johannes Stein, *The Ninth Century*.

117. See Ehrenfried Pfeiffer, *Notes and Lectures Compendium I*, Mercury Press 1991, lecture of December 22, 1946.

118. Copy of Walter Johannes Stein's diary notation in possession of F.L.

119. Dante, *The Divine Comedy*, translated by Laurence Binyon, in *The Portable Dante*, Penguin 1979.

120. Lecture given by Frans Lutters on September 20, 2008; article prepared by Joep Eikenboom.

121. GA 149.

9 781936 367191